*and I predict it will become the bible on Brown Bear hunting in Alaska.*

*... Tony has attained a reputation as the expert on Sheep and Sheep Hunting in Alaska. This book will make him the definitive authority on hunting Alaska's big bears.*

–George McCoy, Ph.D.

*Combining anecdotal material from his own considerable experience as a professional Guide and hunter with a seemingly encyclopedic knowledge of every aspect of the subject, Tony puts together a practical and understandable foundation for successfully accomplishing the ultimate Alaskan dangerous game hunting adventure....*

*It is obvious that his enviable history of involvement with this fascinating type of hunting has resulted from Tony Russ's passion for it. His clear writing style infuses the reader with this passion as it instructs us in the particulars. I would recommend his book without reservation to anyone, novice or expert, seeking the last word on Brown and Grizzly Bear Hunting in Alaska.*

–Tim Shine, Wasilla, Alaska, February, 2004

*Tony Russ' "Bear Hunting in Alaska" is a great compliment to the Alaskana library. This book covers everything from planning to pursuit of Alaska bears. His take on judging a quality bear, stalking, shooting, and field care of a trophy sets the reader's mind at ease by providing the essentials: why, when, where, and how to hunt bears in Alaska! I'm impressed with the knowledge shared in this guidebook. Bravo, Tony!*

–Larry Bartlett, Author / Wilderness Guide

*I would highly encourage anyone interested in bear hunting to first read "Bear Hunting In Alaska." This purely captivating, easy to discern, power-packed book should be considered the encyclopedia of bear hunting in Alaska with extraordinary information from one of Alaska's foremost experts. The abundance of detailed "how-to" secret tips will immensely increase your hunting savvy immediately. Tony Russ's "Bear Hunting In Alaska" delivers the immensely successful techniques and intrigue you won't find anywhere else. And wow, the close encounter hunting action will have you on the edge of your seat with your heart racing, as it did mine.*

–Rich Hackenberg, Author of *Becoming A Great Moose Hunter* and *Moose Hunting In Alaska: The Secrets To Success.*

*You've been advised to "Come loaded for bear!" —*
*Well, if you are armed with this extremely complete book, detailing the bear hunting experience and knowledge of* **Tony Russ***, then you, my friend, are* **"armed to the teeth!"**
–Marc Taylor, Author of *"Hunting Hard...In Alaska!"*

# BEAR HUNTING IN ALASKA

## The Brown & Grizzly Bear Hunter's Guide

### Tony Russ

**Foreword by Dick Gunlogson**
**Photos by numerous Alaskans**

*[signature]*

**Northern Publishing, Wasilla, Alaska**

*Bear Hunting in Alaska: The Brown & Grizzly Bear Hunter's Guide* is one of several comprehensive, how-to manuals produced by TonyRuss.com, dedicated to "Guiding you to Success in the Alaskan Outdoors." Copyright© 2004 by Tony Russ; First Printing 2004.

Published by: Northern Publishing, P.O. Box 871803, Wasilla, AK 99687. www.TonyRuss.com for orders.

Library of Congress Cataloging in Publication Data
Russ, Tony, 1956—
    *Bear Hunting in Alaska: The Brown & Grizzly*
    *Bear Hunter's Guide*
    Includes Index
        1. Hunting--Alaska. 2. Big game hunting--Alaska.
        3. Big game animals--Alaska. I. Title.
        SK49.B37 2004              86-081185
        799.2597
Softcover ISBN 0-9639869-8-8      Hardcover ISBN 0-9741684-0-8
Library of Congress Control Number: Softcover - 2003115995
Library of Congress Control Number: Hardback -2004090756

Produced in the State of Alaska, Printed in the United States of America

Edited by Diane O'Loughlin

Front Cover Photos: Snowshoe-clad hunter by George Wescott
Bear photo placed in foreground by Tony Russ
Back Cover Photo: by George Wescott

# CONTENTS

Foreword
Introduction

Chapter 1 **Excitement** 13

Chapter 2 **Bear Biology** 21

Biological Classification, Trophy Classification, Range of Brown Bears, Physical Characteristics, Behavioral Characteristics, Life History, Diet, Kodiak Brown Bears

Chapter 3 **Hunter Preparation** 41

Physical Training, Cardiorespiratory Conditioning, Stretching, Strength Training, Stamina, Walking, Eating Well, Mental Readiness

Chapter 4 **Bear Hunting Gear** 59

Optics, Footwear, Clothing, Camping, Hunting, Traveling With Gear, Bear Hunter's Gear Checklist

Chapter 5 **When & Where to Hunt** 87

Alaska Game Regulations, Bear Hunting Seasons, Trophy Quality, Places to Hunt

Chapter 6 **Camping in Bear Country** 107

Where to Camp, Pitching Camp, Eating

Chapter 7 **Hunting Bears** 117

Spotting Bears, Spring Hunting, Food Sources, Cruising Shorelines, Stand-Hunting, Snowmachine Hunting

Chapter 8  **Stalking Bears**                                    **155**
    Initial Analysis, Make a Plan, Bears' Eyesight,
    Fooling Their Ears, Beach Stalks, Remain Alert,
    Recovery and Refueling

Chapter 9  **Judging Bears**                                      **171**
    Bear Sizes, Judging Size, Sex Determination,
    Other Trophy Considerations

Chapter 10  **Shooting Bears**                                    **187**
    Sixteen Reasons to Keep Shooting, Calibers &
    Bullets for Bears, Shooting Bears, After the
    Shot

Chapter 11  **Bowhunting Bears**                                  **225**
    Alaska's Bowhunting Laws, Hunting Methods,
    Shooting Bears with a Bow

Chapter 12  **Trophy Care**                                       **237**
    Analysis, The Photo Shoot, Skinning Your Bear,
    Fleshing and Salting

Chapter 13  **Bear Safety**                                       **259**
    DLP Bears, Bear Country Etiquette, Close En-
    counters, Their Moods, Too Close

Chapter 14  **Old Snaggle Tooth**                                 **279**
    World Record Bear, Two Bowhunting Ladies'
    First Bears

References                                                        **283**
Recommended Reading
Photo Credits
Index
Book Order Forms

# FOREWORD

I first became acquainted with Tony Russ quite a number of years ago when he was recommended by a longtime guide on our staff, Bob Jaro, as a highly qualified person to fill an opening on our staff for a bear hunting guide. After meeting with Tony, I was quickly impressed with both his knowledge and experience. I promptly offered him the opportunity to join our staff, which he accepted. That agreement resulted in a number of seasons where he joined our staff on our Alaska Peninsula brown bear hunts.

When I first met Tony, and he joined our staff, it was already time to get ready for the hunting season, so I had little time to really get to "know" Tony other than his knowledge of being well qualified for the job of managing a camp to hunt brown bear. I recall him as being quiet, organized, and self-sufficient as he went about his preparation for the season. Since our hunts are operated on a 1x1 basis and the guide is fully responsible for the hunt upon reaching the field, these qualities impressed me and I knew we had made a good choice.

As that season and then several others went by, I came to know Tony better than just the quiet, efficient guide I knew at the outset of our acquaintance, His hunting, camping, and field abilities, plus his success with taking excellent trophies for happy clients, quickly proved his qualifications as a guide.

It was somewhere along that route, however, that I began to know the "other Tony." I knew he was an avid and very experienced sheep hunter, but, when he asked if it would be okay to bring a copy of his book on sheep hunting, *Sheep Hunting in Alaska*, to the main lodge I became acquainted with Tony Russ, 'Author and Publisher.'

Then, one day when we had a bit of time to do what guides long for, and do best—sit and B.S.—a bit when quiet time occurs around camp, I made a comment about wanting to have some of my pickup sheep horns carved into artwork. I went on to say that I had talked to various artists known to do sheep carvings, but had not found one to whom I wished to make a commitment. Tony, being present and listening to the banter, mentioned quietly, that he did some sheep horn carving. What's this, another Tony?

Anyway, sometime later, I had the opportunity to visit his home and view some of his previous carvings. I promptly went home and gathered up my horns and commissioned him to carve them as he saw fit. Over the years, I have seen a good number of sheep horn carvings, by many highly respected artists, and when I saw the horns he carved for me, I was amazed. They spoke to me of sheep like no other carvings I had ever seen. They also do mean much more to me because they were done by a good friend and colleague rather than some artist I knew only by name.

Other books—*The Manual for Successful Hunters, Alaska Wear, The Quest for Dall Sheep*—followed Tony's book on sheep hunting. Then one day, when we had a chance to visit, he told me he was doing a book on bear hunting and asked if I would be willing to review it when it was finished. I agreed that I would be happy to do so, as maybe I could learn something in the process.

The book is now ready and I have gone over it page by page. The attention to research and detail is typical of Tony's writing and knowledge. Readers will soon realize that this writer is not out to impress them with 'True Stories' of events that make the writer seem larger than life. Rather the reader will see that the information presented in this 'Bear Book' is clearly and concisely presented in a manner that is easy to understand, and just what you need to know and put into practice in the field–and maybe save your life!

Having spent a lot of years with the big bears that Tony writes of, I can only say, if you are going to go bear hunting, **<u>READ IT!</u>**

Dick Gunlogson
Alaskan Master Guide

# INTRODUCTION

I've always been a reader. I remember vividly going through our elementary school library, picking out the outdoor adventure titles one by one. By the time I advanced to junior high, I had exhausted that library of its "worthwhile" books.

I'm not exactly sure when I started reading, but I recently found one indication. This photo (below) shows a young boy reading one of the great publications of my time– *Field & Stream*. I'm not sure of my age in this photo—five or six is my best guess—but I did start reading at a young age.

In high school, I had a very memorable English teacher. She wasn't surprised when I wrote my first book, ten years ago. I still communicate with her, and even asked for her assistance for some grammar intricacies in this book. Mrs. Joan Baxter will always be one of the reasons for my success in life.

As an adult, I read whenever I can, but it is still not enough. There is always more out there I want to know. I cannot imagine going through life and not taking advantage of what others have learned. As for the books I write, I always consult other authors' works to complement what I have learned from my experiences. No hunting book will ever be complete or the final word in hunting–conditions and the animals themselves are constantly changing. However, I research my subjects thoroughly to present the best current knowledge, and so you can go to one reference and not have to duplicate my research time.

Hunting the big bears of Alaska is a great experience. I have been lucky enough to do this many times, as an Alaskan Registered Guide. I've learned a lot about bears, the outdoors, and other hunters. I hope this book enhances your enjoyment and success when hunting these great bears. Good luck.

–Tony Russ, Wasilla, Alaska, Spring 2004

# NOTE TO READER

All Alaskan brown and grizzly bears are now recognized by biologists as one species, *Ursus arctos*. However, as a lifelong Alaskan, I recognize some differences in hunting *coastal brown bears* and *inland grizzly bears*. So, in this book, I will still use the two terms when different hunting techniques are appropriate for coastal versus inland bears. I will also refer to *Kodiak* bears specifically when talking about only this population of bears. When a statement applies to the entire species, I will use the term *brown bears*.

# 1
# Excitement

*"It's not the bears you should worry about, it's that Mack truck with your name on it."* –Tony Russ

Many of us will be crippled or killed by automobiles, but few of us will be harmed by bears. The odds say this is so, but people still worry much more about bear attacks than automobile accidents. Personally, I've always felt that bears pose much less of a threat to us when we are in the field, than automobiles do in our everyday lives. We just don't think about how close we come to death each time a speeding auto goes by us a few feet away as we're standing on a street corner.

To those of us who have been lucky enough to do this many times, bear hunting is addictive. It's not seeing those young bears or the sows with cubs, it's the possibility of spotting those huge, reclusive bears that keeps us coming back each year. Just being in the presence of a king-of-the-woods brown or grizzly bear induces more heart-pounding excitement than any other animal out there. Watching one of these powerful giants eat up ground with its seemingly casual pace, regardless of whether it is downhill or up the side of a mountain, is impressive each and every time it happens. You can just feel the boundless power in that hulk of a body.

On the tenth day of a ten-day Alaskan Peninsula brown bear hunt, the guide I was working for flew overhead as the client and I finished breakfast and suggested to my hunter he could stay longer if he liked. Several other guides from our main camp had finished with their first clients early, and all the second round of clients were out hunting, so I wasn't needed and could stay with my hunter. That's the way hunting works, luck or circumstance has a lot to do with outcome, and the lengthening of this hunt made all the difference for my client.

We had seen several bears, but all had been sows with cubs, or small bears. The evening of the tenth day, after my client's reprieve from the end of his hunt, we spotted a big bear. We only got a few minutes' look as it was waking up for an evening of foraging, but I knew right away it was big. This has always been my experience with big bears– you know right away if they're large. We made a wishful run at the bear that night, but it slipped away into the darkness.

The next morning, we were patiently waiting on our spotting knob as the first light of day illuminated the brush-studded tundra that makes up much of the Alaskan Peninsula. Before the full light of day had flooded the tundra, we spotted him again. This time he was just coming off the beach, three miles from where he disappeared the night before. He had foraged just a little too long and was caught on the open tundra with no "bear condo" to slip into.

He was moving with a purpose as he sought the safety of the first alder bushes he could find. As quickly as we had spotted him and our hopes rose, he disappeared between two clumps of alders. We watched for twenty minutes, but he never reappeared. We were over two miles away with plenty of low hills, streambeds, and alders for the bear to slip behind and make his escape. However, I felt he had found the safety of one of those nearby bear condos. He would now be holed up until darkness again made it safe for him to venture out for another night of adding to his already huge stores of fat, which he would need to survive the long winter ahead.

*At first light, we were watching for the large boar to reappear–and we weren't disappointed.*

Two hours later we had weaved around the smaller alder patches, threaded through the larger ones, and waded across the streams, arriving about two hundred yards downwind of where we last saw the bear. Here we stopped while I repeated my mandatory guide-to-client instructions, which are absolutely necessary when hunting brown bears.

This situation was going to be slightly different than most of my guided brown bear hunts. I felt the bear was sleeping in one of the three alder patches in front of us. We had lost sight of him here, and the next alders weren't for hundreds of yards in any direction. We would be jump-shooting brown bears, one of the most thrilling of all styles of hunting these awesome creatures.

We would walk silently upwind toward one of the alder patches. I would place the hunter on a good shooting bump downwind of the patch. I would then circle around to the upwind side of the patch and try to let the bear get my scent, wake up, and try to escape out the downwind side where the hunter was waiting. Hopefully I could keep the hunter in view at all times and be able to cover him and help with finishing the bear. We would try the smallest patch first.

I settled the hunter on his bump. I walked around the patch slowly and peered into the leafless, but nonetheless dense patch of alders, expecting to see a blur of brown as the bear smelled the terrible scent of humans and hurriedly left his compromised alder patch. I finished circling upwind of the patch, reversed directions and went back around to finish back at the hunter. Nothing in that patch, so we moved to the second.

The second patch was much larger, but still only 30 yards across. We performed the same routine–with the same results. Now I was a little anxious, worrying that maybe the bear had slipped away from us and I had blown the chance at a good bear for my client. The last patch was the largest, 50 yards across. We both hoped (silently) that the bear was in there, fast asleep, unaware of our presence.

I found a five-foot-high mound for the hunter to watch, and shoot, from. I began circling the patch, straining to see brown fur, but the dense alders only let my eyes in just a few short feet. I circled the entire patch, and no bear. I turned to retrace my steps, holding out just a little hope he was sleeping so soundly, my human scent hadn't awakened him. When I was almost back around the upwind side, the snapping started.

At first I thought it was just branches being snapped, then I was sure some of those sounds were two-inch canines being gnashed together by a pissed-off bear that had just been rudely awakened from his daily siesta. I couldn't

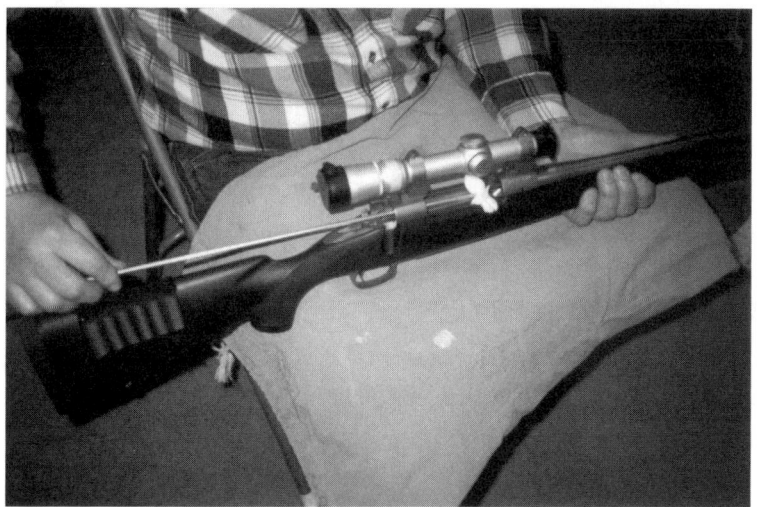

*A smart bear hunter cleans his or her rifle regularly. Jump-shooting bears is no time to have a rifle failure simply because you didn't clean it.*

see anything through the alders, even though the sounds were barely ten yards into the alders. Then a ten-footer stood up, popped his teeth, and swung his paws like a boxer waiting for the opening bell, and he was focused on me. At that point I was pretty sure I was going to have to kill this bear. Then we would have to fill out all that paperwork and deliver the bear to the state.

The client couldn't see the bear from where he was standing because there was a slight rise in the alder patch on his side–partly blocking his view. Suddenly, the bear dropped out of sight and there was silence. I immediately yelled at the client to be ready, that his bear was coming, and not to make a sound. I was hoping I was right and the bear was going toward the client and not me.

Ten seconds passed and I heard nothing. Now I was getting a little worried about the client, whom I couldn't see at times as I paced back and forth. I didn't want to go any farther around the patch to get a better view of the client for fear the bear would slip out my side, so I kept pacing one way to see the client and back the other way to hem in the bear. Thirty seconds passed and the only sounds were my yells at the client to stay put and to not make a sound.

Two minutes passed and finally I saw the bear–right where he had stood up the first time, twenty yards in front of me. He was popping and waving at me again, exactly as he did before. Then he dropped out of sight and the same thing happened–nothing. Then...boom! Several agonizing seconds passed. Then, boom!...and silence. At the first shot I quickly started around toward the client to be in position if I was needed. There were no more shots, but I knew the client's .338 Winchester Magnum held three down, plus the one I had watched him put in the chamber before I left him on the shooting mound. After the second shot, the client disappeared from sight so my mind was racing, wondering if the client was in trouble with a wounded bear in his lap.

I finally caught sight of the client kneeling on his shooting mound, fooling with his rifle. Uh-oh, that could mean a jammed gun and a wounded bear. I yelled over and over again at the client to let me know what was happening and tell me where the bear was, but he couldn't hear me over the twenty-knot wind. I fast-walked toward the client keeping my eyes glued on the alders for the wounded bear. I kept wondering why the client didn't answer me. Had he frozen at the sight of the bear, which was now wounded and coming at him out of my sight? Then I saw the brown hulk in a tundra depression. It wasn't moving and I had my gun on it. What a relief!

The client later explained that he heard the bear popping his teeth the first time and the bear soon appeared just inside the alders near him, but too far in for a clear shot. The bear circled inside the alders and returned to my side to

*This happy client dropped this ten-foot, two-inch brown bear with one shot from his .338 Winchester Magnum at 40 yards, but wisely followed it up with one more insurance round.*

challenge me again. The second time, the bear had come straight out of the patch looking straight ahead as he beelined it for the next alder patch. The client had dropped it with one shot at forty yards and added one more for insurance, as I had instructed.

That was a ten-foot, two-inch bear (but who's counting inches), and it was a relatively young bear, probably not even ten years old. The hide was beautiful with uniform length, silver-tipped, soft hair. We only took that bear because the hunter got a reprieve to hunt another day, which is all he needed. That is how bear hunting—and all hunting—goes, as all you experienced hunters know very well.

When brown bear hunting in Alaska, we live for these few moments of unparalleled excitement. These few moments can make us temporarily forget all those hours and hours of misery and boredom on those spotting knobs; at least until next season when we go out and begin it all over again. But as hunter's luck goes, we are just as likely to see a bear on the first morning of the hunt, as on the first morning of a hunt extension.

I can remember the moments of this hunt nine years ago as well as the hunter can. One of the great aspects of hunting brown bears is all the backup guns–be they friends or guides–live the hunt as much as the hunter. This is why hunters who have come to love pursuing the great Alaskan brown and grizzly bears gladly go along as backup hunters. It doesn't matter that it may cost them thousands of dollars and they will have no chance of a trophy themselves, just being there is a good enough reward. The excitement of a brown bear hunt is everything.

In the next thirteen chapters, I have written everything I've learned about the best ways to hunt the brown and grizzly bears of Alaska. During the writing, I have relived hundreds of moments I enjoyed or endured during bear hunts. Sitting here, they are all great memories I cherish. I hope this book helps you make some great memories for yourself.

*"Life is about timing."* –Carl Lewis

# 2
# BEAR BIOLOGY

*"People's hobbies are more their measure than are their jobs."* –Robert Byrne

For many of us hunters, we have grown up recognizing at least two, and maybe three, different "species" of brown/grizzly bears here in Alaska. Grizzly bears are those bears found inland and in the northern areas of the state. They are known for their bad temperaments, extremely humped shoulders, and sharply curved claws.

Brown bears are the grizzly's larger kin. They are found nearer the coast in more southern areas of Alaska. Their large size is mostly due to their more abundant food supply. What they lack in temperament, they make up for in size. The large brown bears of the Alaska Peninsula are classic examples.

Some of us have even recognized the Kodiak brown bears as separate "species." Their one indisputable attribute is their residence–the Kodiak Archipelago. Of course, their huge size has made them world-renown among hunters and other wildlife enthusiasts alike.

## BIOLOGICAL CLASSIFICATION

Prior to 1950, biologists had as many as nine species classifications for brown bears and 74 species for grizzly bears. In the more recent past, biologists whittled those surprising numbers down to two–one classification for brown bears and one classification for grizzly bears here in Alaska.

*Ursus arctos (formerly Ursus horribilis), the well-known grizzly bear of the Arctic tundra.*

Brown bears were *Ursus middendorffi* and grizzly bears were *Ursus horribilis*. Currently (2004), all brown and grizzly bears in Alaska are classified as one species–*Ursus arctos*. However, the bears of Kodiak are recognized as a subspecies because of their isolation from other bear populations. The one unique physical characteristic they have is their skull has a slightly greater width-to-length ratio than other Alaskan brown/grizzly bears. Kodiak bears are currently classified as *Ursus arctos middendorffi*. They have been geographically isolated for about 12,000 years (2, ADF&G, 2002).

The one other population of brown bears in Alaska that may be geographically isolated is on the Kenai Peninsula. The narrow strip of navigable land between the mainland and the Kenai is somewhat developed and sees quite a bit of human activity. Although there may be little or no influx of other bears into this gene pool, the Kenai brown bears do not have a subspecies designation. As the Kenai gets more and more developed and utilized as a human playground, the health of this population of bears may become threatened.

Even though all Alaskan brown and grizzly bears are now classified by biologists as one species—*Ursus arctos*—as a lifelong Alaskan I recognize some differences in hunting coastal *brown* bears and inland *grizzly* bears. So I will still use the two terms when different hunting techniques are appropriate for coastal versus inland bears. I will also refer to *Kodiak* bears when I am specifically talking about this isolated population of bears.

## TROPHY CLASSIFICATION

For trophy purposes, brown bears and grizzly bears are treated as distinct big game animals. Kodiak bears are grouped with brown bears. The most recognized organization that keeps records of the sizes of North American big game is the Boone and Crockett Club. Their distinction between the two is dependent on where the animal is harvested or where the remains are picked up. The following description comes from Boone & Crockett.

### "Boundaries of the Alaska Brown Bear and Grizzly Bear

The big brown bears are found on Kodiak and Afognak Islands, the Alaska Peninsula, and eastward and southeastward along the coast of Alaska. The smaller interior grizzly is found in the remaining parts of the continent. The boundary between the two was first defined as an imaginary line extending 75 miles inland from the coast of Alaska. Later this boundary was more precisely defined (Figure 2A, page 24) with the current definition as follows:

A line of separation between the larger growing coastal brown bear and the smaller interior grizzly has been devel-

oped such that west and south of this line (to and including
Unimak Island) bear trophies are recorded as Alaska brown
bear.  North and east of this line, bear trophies are recorded
as grizzly bear. The boundary line description is as follows:
Starting at Pearse Canal and following the Canadian-Alaskan boundary northwesterly to Mt. St. Elias on the 141 degree meridian; thence north along the Canadian-Alaskan
boundary to Mt. Natazhat; thence west northwest along the
divide of the Wrangell Range to Mt. Jarvis at the western
end of the Wrangell Range; thence north along the divide
of the Mentasta Range to Mentasta Pass; thence in a general westerly direction along the divide of the Alaska Range
to Houston Pass; thence westerly following the 62nd parallel of latitude to the Bering Sea." ( 8,  Byers, C. Randall and
George A. Bettas, 1999)

## Figure 2A

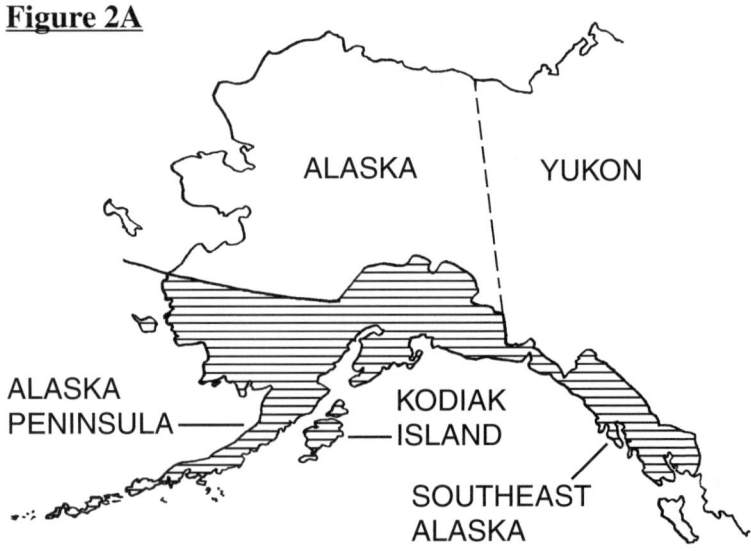

*This map depicts the boundary defined by the Boone & Crockett Club
that separates brown bears (shaded area) from grizzly bears (not
shaded) in Alaska.*

The Pope and Young Club, which recognizes archery-taken animals, uses these same boundaries for brown and grizzly bears entered into their record book.

The Safari Club International has their own set of boundaries. Alaskan brown/grizzly bears taken in units 1-10 and 14-18 are recorded as brown bears. Those bears in units 13-17 and 19-26 are recorded as grizzly bears. This categorization recognizes that the bears of units 11, 13, and 19 are smaller bears due to their inland residence where food supplies are more limited than coastal areas.

## RANGE OF BROWN BEARS

Alaska has more than 95 percent of the U.S. population of brown bears, and 70 percent of the North American population. Those percentages equate to about 30,000 brown bears in Alaska ( 1, ADF&G, 2002). They are residents in most areas of Alaska. The few exceptions are a few islands in southeastern Alaska, the islands beyond Unimak in the Aleutian Chain, and the Bering Sea Islands.

Brown bears can be found in many of the same areas in Alaska as black bears. The glaring exceptions are most of the islands of Southeast. Basically, if brown bears are found on these islands, there aren't any black bears. The reason for this is the brown bears' propensity to eat black bears.

Brown bears are most numerous in the ABC islands (Admiralty, Baranof, and Chicagof) of Southeast, the Kodiak Archipelago, and the Alaska Peninsula. All these locations support strong runs of salmon, which increases both the number and size of brown bears in these areas. This correlation between strong salmon runs and more, and larger bears is seen throughout Alaska.

A brown bear's home range can be as small as a few square miles to as large as a few hundred square miles. Females, especially those with first-year cubs, typically have smaller home ranges than males. When food supplies are plentiful, as they are in many areas of Kodiak Island with numerous salmon streams, home ranges are relatively small. Out of necessity, when food is scarce, home ranges are larger. Interior and northern bears who subsist on widely scattered, opportunistic food sources need to travel large distances daily to find sufficient nutrition to survive.

## PHYSICAL CHARACTERISTICS

The physical characteristics of brown bears are impressive, but not quite as impressive as some claim. The average fall weight of mature males ranges from 500 to 900 lbs. The largest males may stand up to nine feet tall on their hind legs, and about four and one-half feet at the hump on all fours. Mature females are one-half to two-thirds the size and weight of mature males. Extremely large males may weigh as much as 1,500 lbs., but these bears are rare. I have skinned several coastal bears in the ten-foot class and, in my opinion, none was over 1,000 lbs.–even in the fall seasons. But 1,000 lbs. of brown bear is still a very impressive animal. With skulls up to 18 inches long and 12 inches wide, and jaws that can reach around a human head, large brown bears are quite impressive enough without any exaggeration of their size. What is also impressive is that even the largest brown bears begin life at less than one pound.

Adult males can be distinguished from adult females by several characteristics:
  •males have blocky, square jaws and brows when seen in profile;
  •females have more pointed noses and more sloping foreheads than males;
  •males' neck lengths are between two-thirds and three-thirds the lengths of their heads;

*These two boars have the typical long necks, dark color, and blocky facial profiles that distinquish them as males.*

•females' neck lengths are less than two-thirds the lengths of their heads;

•males have more widely flaring and wider shoulders than females;

•males are usually darker in color, females are lighter;

•and adult males are typically larger than adult females in any given area.

(*for a more detailed discussion of distinguishing male brown bears from female brown bears, see Chapter Nine, "Judging Bears")

In the spring, brown bears weigh 30-40 percent less than when they are heaviest–right before denning in late fall. They gain weight rapidly during the summer, particularly when they enjoy several months of a protein-rich food supply like salmon. In many areas, bears begin eating salmon as early as June when the king salmon arrive. As the summer progresses, they feed on sockeye, humpy, and dog salmon, finishing with silver salmon in October, or as late as November in some areas. This four- to six-month period with a nonstop, plentiful supply of protein-rich food is what grows the huge bears of the Alaska Peninsula, the Kodiak Archipelago, and southeastern Alaska. During this time, large males can gain up to several pounds per day as they fatten up to waddling stage just before denning for winter.

In the wild, brown bears may live up to 34 years, although an average male typically lives to about 22 years and a female to about 26 years (1, ADF&G, 2002). Brown bears are sexually mature at three to five years of age; northern grizzlies may not produce a litter until seven years of age (1, ADF&G, 2002).

Brown bears are known for their quickness–they can reach speeds up to 35 m.p.h. almost immediately from a dead stop. This means they can cover 150 feet in three seconds from a standstill.

Their strength is also legendary. Witnesses have seen adult male bears, engaged in battles, that actually picked up their adversaries by the neck and shook them like rag dolls. I can remember one of my early moose-hunting trips to the Brooks Range when we spotted a fresh moose kill on an inside corner of a small river. We stayed clear of the site, but did spot the large male that apparently had made the kill. As we were flying out of the area, we saw where the bear had drug the moose across the river and into the alders. What so impressed me was that this bear weighed less than the moose, yet it drug the moose 100 feet across the river and then up a steep, ten-foot-high bank covered with alders. And the bear had only his teeth with which to grasp the moose–strong jaws, strong neck, and a very strong bear!

Brown bears in Alaska range from very light, cream-colored individuals, to the classic Toklat grizzlies with light, silver-tipped backs and very dark brown legs, to all-dark

*This congregation of bears fishing for salmon is a common sight on many Alaskan rivers as bears fatten up for hibernation during the long winter ahead.*

bears–sometimes almost black. During one fall bear season on the Alaska Peninsula, we watched one eight-footer that we first thought was a caribou because of its almost-white neck and brown saddle. My hunter passed on this bear on two occasions because it wasn't large enough, but I would have loved a hide with that coloration–no matter what the size. On another guided hunt in the Talkeetna's, we spotted a sow with three cubs, one of which was almost completely white from nose to tail. Unfortunately, I don't think that bear had much chance of surviving to adulthood because it was so easy for predators to spot. A bear like that also would have been a unique, beautiful trophy, regardless of its size as an adult.

Distinguishing between brown/grizzly bears and black bears is not always a simple matter, particularly in field conditions when seconds may be all the time available for observation. Although none of these are always absolute evi-

*Even this young brown bear displays the prominent hump, dished face, and large head that distinquish brown bears from black bears.*

dence of species by themselves, the useful characteristics of each are:

•brown bears usually have a more prominent hump between their shoulders than black bears–"The musculature and bone structure of the hump are adaptations for digging and for attaining bursts of speed necessary for capture of moose or caribou for food." (1, ADF&G, 2002);

•brown bears have dished faces, black bears have "Roman" noses;

•brown bears have long, straight claws—over two and one-half inches—designed for digging roots or digging out the burrows of small mammals; black bears have shorter, curved claws—usually under two inches—which allow them to climb trees better than brown bears;

•brown bears' muzzles are usually the same color as their coat, black bears often have tan or brown muzzles regardless of coat color;

•brown bears have larger heads in relation to their bodies, and smaller ears in relation to their heads, than black bears;

•brown bears, mostly older individuals, often have white streaks along their claws, black bears seldom do;

•and in brown bears the "...upper rear molar is larger than one and one-quarter inches along the jaw line, and on black bears it is less than one and one-quarter inches." (11, Gilchrist, 1989)

Although none of these characteristics by themselves will categorize every bear, hunters can use them in concert to easily identify each species in the field.

## BEHAVIORAL CHARACTERISTICS

In general, brown bears are solitary creatures and avoid living around other bears. The exceptions to this are females with offspring, mating partners, and bears gathered near very high concentrations of food.

Bears have low population densities in Alaska, ranging from one bear per square mile to one bear per three hundred square miles. Mountainous areas, typical of inland or northern habitats, usually have the lowest densities. Coastal areas and many islands have the highest densities. Kodiak Island has about one bear per square mile. Areas between the two extremes, which also have intermediary quantities of food, support bear densities between the two extremes. Densities of 15-20 bears per square mile are typical of inland areas with good yearly berry crops and a limited supply of salmon on which bears can feed.

These densities are food-dependent and vary in correlation with the food supply. The densities are often season-dependent as the food supply varies. Spawning salmon and ripe berries are two of the more common foods that concentrate bears seasonally. On some "fishable" rivers with large numbers of salmon, dozens of brown bears can be seen from one vantage point. These high densities are temporary, occurring only at the peak of the salmon runs. At other times, hunters in these areas may be hard-pressed to spot even a single bear in a day's time. Bears are only present as long as a food supply lasts. The result is that bears spend most of their time on one percent of their territory–the one percent that contains their food.

Bears are not territorial. They do have traditional home ranges and these may overlap with other bears' home ranges. Although brown bears do not defend territories, they will vigorously defend their food, their offspring, and their breeding partners.

Bears do not share food. Even sows do not share food or offer it to their cubs. The cubs have to take the food they want and defend it from their sibling(s). So they are conditioned from an early age to take food they want and defend it. This trait to take and defend food is one of the greatest sources of conflict between bears and man.

Brown bears are normally diurnal (active during the day), but will become more nocturnal when other bears or people move in on their food or space. Large boars that have been hunted are the most likely bears to become nocturnal. The brown bears of the Alaska Peninsula are good examples of this. Many large boars are completely nocturnal during the hunting season after learning, in their younger years, about the threat hunters pose.

Although bears do not share food, when food becomes very concentrated (like when salmon plug a stream or mul-

*These two bears are feeding in close proximity, but using their body language to avoid fighting–which may cause crippling or lethal injuries to both.*

tiple bears find a beached whale), they may feed in very close proximity. To express their moods and avoid unnecessary fights in feeding situations like these, during the breeding season, and when chance meetings between bears occur, brown bears have developed ways to communicate and a hierarchial social structure.

Like many species of animals, when two bears meet they first size up each other. They look at physical size, sex, temperament, and mood. Head wagging is a sign of slight irritation. This can lead to gargling noises, teeth-popping, and bluff charges as signs of high irritation and willingness to fight–just like they are when bears encounter humans.

Large, aggressive bears and sows defending cubs are more dominant over smaller or more passive bears. Complex, dominance hierarchies develop around active salmon streams when numerous bears encounter each other on a daily basis. This structure prevents unnecessary injury and death by establishing and maintaining which bears have priority fishing rights, or which bears have to give way along trails to and from fishing and bedding areas.

Some bears are just more prone to fight than others. One bear we took in southeastern Alaska was covered with scars, even though he was relatively young. It was early spring, but he even had fresh scars from that season. He was also one of the fattest bears—covered with four inches of fat from head to tail—I have ever seen, spring or fall. I surmised that he just liked to eat and was willing to fight for it. He wasn't the largest bear in the area by any means, but he looked like he obtained more than his share of the food.

*This sow lost a large chunk of hide and muscle from the side of her head, presumably in a fishing dispute. Although their social structure helps reduce these injuries, bears are still aggressive creatures so fights and the resulting injuries do occur.*

Brown bears' denning habits in Alaska are generally known, but their hibernation physiology is not totally understood. In late fall, October or November, most Alaska brown bears den and hibernate until April, May, or even June for some sows with cubs. A small percentage of bears on Kodiak and other islands come out sporadically during winter or don't den at all in mild winters.

Bears choose den sites that will allow them the most uninterrupted sleep until food is once again available in the spring. Pregnant sows tend to den first and come out last in spring with their cubs. Large boars are usually the last to den and the first to reappear in the spring. Exceptions to this are young bears who don't have enough experience to choose den sites that keep them hibernating until food is available in the spring. Bears that emerge from hibernation before ample food is available don't have the best chance of survival. Food is scarce and predation rates on these smaller bears are high. This is one of the reasons young bears, ages three to five, have a high mortality rate.

Hibernating brown bears have reduced heart rates, body temperatures, and metabolic rates. They have no need to eat or drink while in this state. In the northern areas of Alaska, some bears may hibernate for up to seven months. Yet, when they emerge in the spring, they have lost little muscle tone or bone mass. Understanding how a bear's physiology accomplishes these feats could have some real benefits for medical science and human health issues.

## LIFE HISTORY

Brown bears in Alaska mate from May to July–with the most activity occurring in early June. Males often mate with more than one female during the season. After breeding for up to ten days, the pair separates. They do not have any strong mating ties. During this time, males and barren females move throughout their home range looking for breeding partners.

Although brown bears are supposed to breed with only one partner at a time, I swear I saw an exception one spring. I was hiking just south of Anchorage and watched three bears "playing" on a snowfield. I watched them for half an hour or more and realized there were two sows "sharing" one boar. This is not supposed to happen, but perhaps they were young, twin sows with strong sibling ties who wouldn't have it any other way.

Once a sow is pregnant, her fertilized egg then enters a state of delayed implantation for the summer. In fall, the egg will begin to grow again just before the pregnant sow dens for the winter. The cubs are born in January or February in the den while the mother is still in a state of hibernation. Litters range from one to four in size, with two cubs being the most common. They are hairless, have closed eyes, and weigh less than one pound each. The cubs suckle for a few months in the den and emerge with the sow in spring.

Cubs weigh about 15-20 pounds when they come out of the den. Typically, sows with first-year cubs remain near their dens for a week or more as the cubs grow stronger and adapt to the "outside" world. "Sows are sometimes seen with five or six cubs in tow, probably due to adopting cubs from other litters." (2, ADF&G, 2002)

Most cubs remain with their mothers for two years. During this time, their mortality rate is over 25 percent. In areas with high bear densities, like Kodiak Island, cannibalism is a leading cause of death. Most of this occurs in spring when large boars seek out cubs for a source of high-protein food. Boars will even dig out hibernating sows to get the cubs they can smell beneath the surface of the snow.

Cubs almost always den with their sow the first winter. They do not den with their sow the second winter, but may choose a den site very near their sow. In areas of limited food sources, cubs will sometimes remain with their

*At popular fishing sites, cubs usually stay very close to mom, and they should. One of the main causes of cub mortality is being eaten by large boars.*

mothers for up to five years. During this time, sows usually won't breed. When a sow with cubs does come into estrus in spring, she will usually chase away her cubs (at least two-year olds). On their own for the first time and looking for food and their own space, these juvenile, uneducated bears are often the ones that have conflicts with humans.

Depending on the food supply in an area, sows have cubs every three to five years, and up to seven years for bears in northern, demanding habitats. Coastal sows tend to have cubs more frequently than inland bears, which have shorter "growing" seasons and hibernate longer.

## DIET

Brown bears are omnivores; their diet consists of a variety of plants and animals. Alaskan bears subsist mostly on salmon, roots, grasses, sedges, berries, ground squirrels, large marine and land mammals, and carrion. They can kill large animals, but many bears are up to 90 percent vegetarian because of where they live. Inland grizzlies tend to have a more vegetarian diet because their access to salmon is limited. They are also smaller on average, which makes them less capable of killing large ungulates like moose and caribou.

Most brown bears are inefficient hunters, although many adult bears will take advantage of young moose and caribou calves in spring. Some large boars do become proficient at killing adult moose, but they are the exception. Inland grizzlies do regularly take ground squirrels and an occasional caribou. Most of the carrion in bears' diets is killed by other predators, by accidents, or by Alaska's harsh winters.

There are two reasons bears tend to wait a few days before eating any animals they do kill themselves. The first is that bears may not be able to digest freshly killed red meat very well. By waiting, the now-rotting meat is better utilized by their digestive system. The second reason is to let the meat be infested by maggots, which then serve as an easily digestible, high-quality source of protein.

When bears first emerge in spring they, out of necessity, feed on the first foods available. Coastal bears feed on beach grasses, sedges, roots they dig on the first-exposed, south-facing hillsides, carrion, and—for large boars—bear cubs. Coastal bears often cruise the beaches in search of large, dead sea mammals. A beached whale will often attract a dozen or more bears for weeks as they take advantage of this excellent source of protein and calories. Inland bears feed on roots and grasses from the first-exposed slopes, ground squirrels, and any carrion they can find. Slopes where bears have been digging for roots are easily identified by the numerous one to three-foot craters–each exposing fresh earth.

Brown bears have adapted to find the most nutritious foods, at the best time of year, and use the best parts of that

*In Alaska, the relationship between salmon and bears is as strong as that between caribou and wolves. Where you find one, you will almost certainly find the other.*

food. Forbs and grasses are used mostly in the spring when they are growing rapidly and are the most nutritious (for bears). When salmon are plentiful, bears first eat the eggs, brains, and then flesh. The first parts of any fresh moose, caribou, or deer kills that bears eat are the internal organs. Berries are most often eaten when they are fully ripe and their sugar content is at its peak.

## KODIAK BROWN BEARS

Since Kodiak brown bears are recognized as a distinct subspecies—*Ursus arctos middendorffi*—and since they have a reputation among hunter(s), I am including a separate section devoted to them. Kodiak bears live exclusively on islands of the Kodiak Archipelago. Kodiak Natives traditionally hunted Kodiak bears for food, tools, and clothing. Kodiak bears were even commercially hunted throughout the 1800s. Cattle ranchers on Kodiak waged war with the bears for 200 years, even shooting them from airplanes to reduce their numbers at one point. Current management practices to protect the bear population began in 1941 with the creation of the Kodiak National Wildlife Refuge.

Today, there are about 3,000 Kodiak bears with a density of one bear for every one or two square miles-a high density for brown bears in Alaska. They also have a small home range size because of the rich variety of foods present on Kodiak. Despite widespread hunting pressure (under a permit system) and an annual take of about 170 bears, their numbers are stable or slowly increasing. This is due to good management of the bears as well as well-managed salmon populations. Kodiak National Wildlife Refuge and the Alaska Department of Fish and Game cooperatively conduct bear management, research, and habitat protection.

*"Thinking is the hardest work there is, which is probably the reason so few engage in it."* –Henry Ford

# 3
# HUNTER PREPARATION

*"...nothing gets you closer to your visions than intense exercise." –Rob Powell*

A hunter's success often depends on his or her physical and mental readiness. Some hunters choose to ignore these aspects of their preparation, but any experienced hunter or guide can attest to the positive correlation between fitness and success in the field. Physical and mental preparation are even more important when you plan to hunt brown bears in Alaska.

One of my spring, Alaska Peninsula brown bear hunts was a good example. My client was a slightly overweight, late-fifties Mexican man with short legs. After spotting a large boar coming our way in early afternoon, we started moving up a riverbed toward the bear. We quickly covered two miles on a slightly uphill grade. We were wearing hip boots and carrying light packs and rifles. The terrain then became much more taxing as we left the riverbed. We ran into soft snow and steeper terrain. We couldn't afford to slow down for fear the bear would suddenly veer off course and we would lose him.

My client was huffing and puffing hard, but kept up with me every step of the way. As we finally closed in on the bear, it suddenly changed direction and cut across our path. We had to step up our pace to quickly cut it off before our opportunity literally ran away from us. The snow got softer and the slope steeper, but we were able to get into position just in time for a clean kill.

This client was not the most ideal candidate for climbing snow-covered hills in hip boots. His physical conditioning was barely adequate, but his superb mental toughness made up for what his body lacked. If he would have been in better shape, we would have had some margin for error—in case the bear veered sooner, or to have more time to get settled before the shot—but he was prepared *enough* to take this beautiful, nine and one-half foot bear.

*This client was pushed to his physical and mental limits during the stalk on this nine-foot, six-inch Alaskan Peninsula brownie.*

We are each a unique combination of physical and mental attributes, and all of us can improve our abilities in each of these areas. To the extent we can do that in preparation for a bear hunt, we can improve our chances of bagging the trophy we are after.

## PHYSICAL TRAINING

Physical training for brown bear hunting in Alaska is mostly directed at being able to walk hard for at least two hours. That is what an optimistic bear hunter should be able to do–at the least. If you can do that, you are prepared for many of the good opportunities that will be presented. Of course, if you can do more than that minimum, your chances of success improve. If you can walk hard, wearing hip boots, carrying a light pack and your rifle, over rough terrain, for *four* hours straight, your chances of capitalizing on good opportunities go up significantly.

With that goal—walking hard for two to four hours—in mind, I train for bear hunting in a similar fashion to how I train for most Alaskan hunting. The four areas of my physical training program are:

- •cardiorespiratory conditioning
- •stretching for flexibility
- •strength training
- •stamina training

I explain in great detail how to design these four parts of physical training for Alaskan hunting in two of my previous books: *Sheep Hunting in Alaska* and *The Manual for Successful Hunters.* They are available through my website—www.TonyRuss.com—where I also have the most recent information (as free downloads) about preparation for Alaskan hunting. For this discussion, I will briefly outline the most important aspects of physical training for bear hunting in Alaska.

## CARDIORESPIRATORY CONDITIONING

Cardiorespiratory (cardio) conditioning simply refers to training your heart and lungs to be more efficient, so these organs can supply enough oxygen to your muscles to keep you moving for a long time. This is the single most important aspect of physical training for an Alaskan bear hunt.

Indoor "cardio" work is typically done in exercise rooms on treadmills, elliptical gliders, stair steppers/climbers, stationary bicycles, rowing machines, or similar apparatus. Their common purpose is to require you to use large muscle groups and make you breathe hard for a long time. The minimum exercise time needed to get good results is about 60 minutes per week. Doing 20 minutes of cardio exercise three times per week is a standard pattern for beginners. However, you can achieve very similar results by doing 60 minutes of the same exercise per week–no matter how you break up the time. Doing more than 60 minutes will benefit your cardiorespiratory system even more.

*Hiking with family or friends is one of the best ways to prepare for Alaskan bear hunting. Almost any outdoor activity that involves continuous motion will help prepare you for the physical and mental demands of a hunt. By climbing hills regularly, you will know you have the ability to do so when the time comes during your hunt.*

For brown bear hunters, who need to walk hard (or run) to be successful during a hunt, the best choices of indoor cardio work would be the treadmill and the stepper/climbers. In addition to improving your cardiovascular system, using these exercise apparatus will work the muscles most commonly used on a bear hunt. For outdoor cardio work, walking, running, and climbing are the best choices for bear hunters who also want to train their walking muscles used most often during a hunt.

## STRETCHING

The ten to fifteen minutes immediately following a cardio workout is an ideal time to stretch. Some people think of stretching as the first thing to do *before* a workout, but this can often injure cold, stiff tissues. Stretching is much more useful as a post-workout activity. After a workout, muscles and joints are warm, pliable, and able to accommodate the greater range of motion you are trying to achieve by stretching. By stretching *after* a workout, you are more likely to achieve greater flexibility and range of motion, which will prevent the likelihood and severity of future injuries.

Stretching is the most common method used to increase both muscle flexibility and joint mobility. Retaining the complete range of motion in each of your joints, regardless of how minor it seems, is vital for each joint to remain healthy. Once a joint has a limited range of motion, the related muscles—which then cannot stretch as much because the joint restricts them—will become shorter and less pliable, and then restrict that joint even more. This begins a vicious cycle, where shortened muscle tissue restricts joint movement, which loses its range of motion, which then causes the muscle tissue to shorten even more, and on and on.

When this happens, our human bodies look OLD–regardless of our age. We walk around hunched over, with short stiff steps. We can't bend, twist or reach like normal human bodies were intended to. Stretching is the best way to minimize this loss of flexibility and mobility, which can start as soon as we become adults–in our twenties.

You can do very simple, natural stretches like a wake-up stretch–the kind that just feels good after a short nap or overnight slumber. Or, you can go to the other extreme and delve into one of the many types of yoga, the newer Pilates-type exercise routines which are similar to yoga, or just go through a standard stretching routine on a regular basis.

Stretching is a very natural activity for all animals. Dogs and cats are obvious examples. They always stretch whenever they get up from a nap–which for my pets is a dozen or more times a day. We also feel the same urge to stretch. It feels good to stretch, because it's good for our health. I highly recommend you stretch whenever you get the urge (if it is an appropriate time). If you want to learn the basics correctly or get serious about stretching, I also recommend getting some form of instruction–from either a trainer, video, or manual. One manual I recommend is *Stretching* (see Recommended Reading) by Bob Anderson.

However you stretch, there are some important points to remember to achieve maximum benefit and avoid injuries–and stretching injuries are some of the most common sports-related injuries because most people don't stretch properly:

•warm up before any serious stretching session–just a few minutes of walking, jogging, or using a treadmill is all that's necessary;

•always move slowly whenever stretching–quick movements are invitations to muscle, ligament, and joint injuries;

•you can intersperse stretching during an exercise session (like when you are climbing a mountain) or stretch after you are done exercising–but before your muscles and joints cool down;

*For those who want to continue hunting into their late sixties, like this bear hunter has, stretching is virtually a prerequisite. This hunter is wearing hip boots because the odds are, when he spots that bear of a lifetime, it will be on the other side of the braided river, and he won't want to lose any time changing footwear.*

•breathe deeply and slowly during the stretch to get the most out of each movement;

•as you move into a stretch, pay close attention to the muscle(s) involved–when you feel a *slight* pull, stop, and wait for the muscle to relax before trying to go further;

•you should never feel real pain during a stretch;

•an effective stretch can be held between two and one hundred seconds (it depends on your purpose and the amount of time available–even two seconds can help, although six seconds is a practical minimum for most people using standard stretching methods);

•and don't compete when stretching–do each stretch just the right way for *your* body.

Improper stretching can do you more harm than good. Some of the most nagging injuries I have are the results of poor stretching. I have an eight-year-old shoulder injury and a partially torn Achilles tendon from overzealous stretching. Stretching—done properly—should extend our abilities and longevity in the hills–not cut our hunting time short.

## STRENGTH TRAINING

Most activities during a brown bear hunt don't require more than an ordinary amount of strength. There is one exception to that generalization–packing a large bear hide. Although there are a few ways to accomplish this superhuman feat without being superhuman (see the discussion about sleds and travois in Chapter Four, "Bear Hunting Gear"), in most situations brute strength is necessary.

One of my clients—a healthy, under-forty type who was instructed to bring a daypack—was little help when the time came to pack his ten-foot, Alaskan Peninsula brown bear. His daypack turned out to be the tiniest, teardrop-style pack I've ever seen. It would barely hold his lunch and water bottle. I even had to carry his raincoat on the few days he wasn't wearing it (fall hunts on the Peninsula can be wet from start to finish).

I ended up leaving the bear skull in the ten-foot, two-inch hide because our pick-up plane was waiting about 800 yards away. I had a single-compartment, oversize pack, but

*Large bear hides are amazingly heavy. Add the awkwardness of an uncooperative bear head, and packing them can tax the strongest of hunters. This hunter is as happy for his success, as he is that the pack is finally over.*

it still wasn't enough for the hide and head. The head ended up sitting on top of my pack for that grueling, non-stop march over soggy muskeg. With my hip boots sticking with every step, and having to lean forward to balance the 140-pound load, I was—as he put it—"red-lining" (my engine) after the first 400 yards.

The head kept sliding further and further out of my pack and threatening to come over my head. By the time I was halfway to the plane, my neck was cramping from blocking the bear head from sliding over the top. We couldn't stop because I didn't want to keep my pilot waiting–you always want to stay on your pilot's good side when your supply of fresh food and your place on his priority list depend on his attitude toward you. I made it to the plane without overheating and blowing a gasket, but I didn't have anything left. An extra 10 percent of strength would have saved me a lot of suffering over that 800 yards.

Packing a large bear hide—which can weigh over 100 pounds without the head—is the one circumstance that requires one member of your hunting party to have exceptional brute strength. If you have a packer, great. If not, you must plan on how to get the hide back to camp, or to where your mechanical transportation can pick it up.

If you need to work on strength in preparation for a hunt, select exercises that work your large leg and back muscles. These muscles will be the most useful for packing a large hide, or just for the hard walking needed to stalk a bear. The most important rule to remember whenever you work out for strength is: intensity and focus will help more than time or repetitions. An intense, short workout (less than 45 minutes), where you focus on each muscle as it is trained, will build more strength in a shorter time than long, casual workouts. Intensity and focus seem simple enough, but they are the keys in the weight room.

Older hunters may need more strength work than many younger hunters. As we age, the average person loses about one percent of their muscle mass per year, which equates to about five pounds per decade. Proper strength training with weights can slow down this loss tremendously and keep us hunting successfully into our later years.

For more reading on strength training, I recommend *Boomers Really Can Put Old on Hold, Staying Fit Over Fifty,* and *Strength Training Past 50* (see Recommended Reading).

*This bear hunter called himself a 'Flatlander from Georgia' who couldn't climb much. After spotting this nine-footer four miles away on a snowfield, I kept urging him to climb 'just a little more' to get a better look at the bear. Eventually, we reached the bear and the hunter took home a great trophy. In this case, he had the physical ability, but his mind simply wasn't aware of that fact. Preseason preparation will convince you what you can and can't do.*

## STAMINA

Stamina for bear hunters equates to the ability to walk hard for hours. This is best developed by first attaining a good level of fitness—a fitness you already have or have attained by several months of training—then exercising strenuously for several hours, or a whole day. Cardio work— indoors or outdoors—is great for this. When you have exercised vigorously for hours and you are getting really tired,

then go hard for a while longer. By pushing yourself beyond the point of being tired, even to the point of exhaus-
tion, your stamina limits will be expanded.

You may not need any real stamina on some bear hunts.
A hunt may just require one or two short stalks to produce
your trophy bear. You may also be lucky enough to find a
bear kill and just sit until your bear comes to you. However,
if your hunt involves a long day with one difficult, failed
stalk in the morning, then another exhausting stalk late in
the day, the amount of stamina you have could very well be the
deciding factor in the success of your hunt. The way I see it,
having extra stamina helps me enjoy just about everything I do
in my life, as well as improves my chances in the field.

## WALKING

If you don't do anything else besides walking in preparation for a bear hunt, you can fare pretty well. Walking is
the one best exercise I have found for all of my hunting, as
well as for my general health. Additionally, walking works
the muscles most used on a hunt.

One of my bear hunting clients was a healthy looking
man in his early sixties. The day he took his bear had been
a long one. After a long, uphill climb in pursuit of the bear,
we had a long, downhill pack through difficult terrain filled
with thick alders. Although I can often out-walk clients carrying only their rifles, even when I carry a full pack, this
client was different. I thought he would be a pretty tired,
old man after the long day and I would be the leader down
the mountain. Instead, he left me in his dust from the beginning. I even let him go ahead to find the best route because
I was having such a difficult time fighting my way through
the alders, while he looked completely rested.

When I asked him his secret, he told me he walked
three miles every day–sometimes twice a day. He had done

this for years, which I know from personal experience makes a big difference. He was in great shape for sixty-plus years old.

If you do walk for conditioning, you can also carry a pack for at least the last few months before a hunt. This will help if you have to pack that ten-foot bear hide, but it will also help when you are just carrying your rifle and day pack on those long, hurried stalks sometimes needed to cut off a fast-moving bear.

*The corollary to being able to spot bears at great distances–is being prepared to walk great distances to stalk them.*

You should also try to find any convenient, hilly terrain available to you. My neighborhood has only a couple small rises, but I do try to push hard up those. I also visit a nearby "butte" whenever I can for real climbing exercise. In place of hilly, outdoor terrain, you can use any convenient stairs (tall, office-building staircases are a favorite here in Alaska) to mimic the natural uphills so common in Alaska.

For those who want to learn the finer points of walking or hiking for exercise, I highly recommend *The Complete Walker IV*, by the guru of modern walking and hiking–Colin Fletcher (see Recommended Reading).

## EATING WELL

If you go to the effort of physical conditioning, get the most out of it by eating well. I have often heard and read that up to 80 percent of the results of any physical conditioning you do is determined by the food you eat. My personal experience makes me believe this is probably a true statement. I definitely believe what you eat during a hunt dramatically affects how you perform physically and mentally.

If you aren't sure how important food is, try a test. Pick a time of day when your energy typically lags the most. Then, for the next week, eat one of the many nutritionally "balanced" energy/protein bars (I like Balance, Luna, Zone, and Clif bars) during this time. Don't eat anything else for about two hours afterward. Unlike a chocolate/candy bar, your energy level should go up and stay up for about one to two hours. These bars have a "balance" of carbohydrates, fat, and protein that keeps your body fueled consistently for as long as the bar's 200-300 calories last.

For comparison, try eating a candy bar or doughnut during your low-energy period and note any differences. You will most likely feel great for ten to twenty minutes, then be looking for another snack to get you going again.

Eating a balanced diet during training or in the field has the same effects over the course of each day as the balanced energy bars do over an hour or two. Eating a poor

*Eating and drinking well will keep bear hunters hunting hard until they find that one bear they have been looking for. Even Spartan camps like this one can provide high-quality food for those who understand what hard-working hunters need to keep going day after day.*

diet is comparable to putting 50-octane gas in a motorized vehicle that is made to run on 80-octane gas. Most of us don't water down the gas for our vehicles, because they would run poorly–at best. Why water down your body's fuel by eating a poor diet and causing your performance to suffer in everything you do?

Drinking sufficient quantities of water is just as important as eating a balanced diet. An estimated 75 percent of Americans are chronically dehydrated. Even mild dehydration can slow down your metabolism by three percent. The number one cause of daytime fatigue is lack of water. Don't reduce your performance by not drinking enough water. Eight to ten glasses per day is needed by the average adult, so if you want to have the best chance at bagging your trophy bear, you should plan on getting at least that much water, and probably more.

## MENTAL READINESS

If you *know* you are physically ready for your brown bear hunt, you have taken a large step toward being mentally ready. Brown bear hunting is the most exciting, and unnerving, adventure many people will have during their lifetimes. It is best to address and improve your mental readiness well before the hunt–if you want to have the highest chance of success.

Besides being physically ready, it will benefit you tremendously to have absolute confidence in your gun, your loads, your ability to shoot your weapon accurately to your predetermined maximum distance, your understanding of where to aim and when to stop shooting (when the bear stops moving!), and your backup person. These items will be addressed in Chapters Ten and Eleven–"Shooting Bears" and "Bowhunting Bears." Studying those chapters will help your confidence and mental readiness greatly.

You must also be ready for the rigors of your hunt. Bear hunting often involves long hours of sitting or standing and glassing meticulously and patiently. The more meticulously you search the tundra and bushes and the more patiently you stay in one place all day, the more likely you are to spot your trophy bear. Some hunts may require you to sit and watch a kill site or a salmon stream for endless hours. Others involve long hours on boats as you cruise the shoreline, watching meticulously for bears or parts of bears. Regardless of the style of bear hunting you do, it is vital to your success that you prepare yourself for long hours of careful watching. Planning for the long, sometimes boring, hours will make them much easier to endure successfully.

*Preparation is the key to many aspects of bear hunting. Feeling physically and mentally ready is absolutely necessary when you meet a bruin like this Boone & Crockett, Kodiak bruin (28 9/16 B&C).*

As a guide, I have seen bear hunters arrive in the field in all states of physical and mental readiness. It is obvious to me how physical preparation and mental readiness affect a brown bear hunter's chances of success. These two factors sometimes even affect how large a trophy a client will take home. Luck can always play a part in hunting, and a few unprepared hunters were just plain lucky when it came to brown bears. But, being prepared often brings "luck" your way.

*"Successful people are very lucky. Just ask any failure."* –Michael Levine

*Large brown bears have very impressive skulls.*

# 4
# BEAR HUNTING GEAR

*"The Future Belongs to Those Who Prepare for It."*
—Ralph Waldo Emerson

Some of the choices you make about bear hunting gear will affect your comfort level while hunting, and some will actually affect your hunting success. Since brown/grizzly bear hunting occurs in many different terrains in Alaska with various weather patterns, it is impossible to identify one single gear list for every possible bear hunt in this immense state. However, there are some general rules to follow and some items that should go with any bear hunter.

One of the basic rules is that your gear should be wind- and water-proof. That rule basically applies whenever you say hunting and Alaska in the same sentence, and most brown bear hunts are even windier and wetter than the average Alaskan hunt.

## OPTICS

Brown bear hunters typically spend many hours a day behind their binoculars. Their ability to spot bears with their binoculars is the single most significant factor in their success.

Rule number two for brown or grizzly bear hunters in Alaska is to take the best waterproof binoculars you can afford to bring. If your binoculars fail the waterproof test in the field, the odds are you will go home empty-handed. If you are sitting on a salmon stream or cruising a shoreline, you may still succeed, but why take the risk just to save a few dollars by buying cheap binoculars. Quality binoculars will last for twenty years if cared for properly, and they can be used on hunts of every kind, everywhere in the world, all year long. They are a bargain even though the initial cash outlay may be shocking.

Buy at least eight-power binoculars, and ten-power are often better. For ten-power binoculars to be effective, they must also have larger objective lenses (the bigger end) to let in more light. That means they will weigh more–a lot more. The difference in weight between 8x30's and 10x50's can be more than double.

I have a pair of Swarovski 8x30's with a wide, neo-prene neck strap that weigh 25 ounces. A pair of 10x50's will weigh about twice as much. Although heavier binoculars can be easier to hold steady when glassing, over the course of a day they can wear out most hunters' shoulders. If a hunter is resting his shoulders most of the time because he can't hold his binoculars up for more than a few minutes, he will miss the many bears that are visible for only a few seconds. It would be better to have binoculars you can hold up to your eyes much longer than a higher-powered set that is hanging from your neck most of the time while your shoulders rest.

Next to being waterproof, the most important aspect of a bear hunter's binoculars is the quality of the lenses. You will see more bears and feel less eye fatigue with good quality optics. A pair of good quality, waterproof 8x30 binoculars is great for most hunters looking for bears. If you can handle the weight of 10x50's for hours and hours, that would be slightly better, but not vital to your success. Lens quality is more important than power.

*High-quality, waterproof binoculars of at least eight power are the most important piece of gear a bear hunter can have. Spotting bears is what bear hunting is all about, and you will spot more bears with better binoculars.*

I once was in the field with several hunters, all with different makes and models of binoculars. It was amazing how much difference there was between brands in the optical quality. My Swarovski 8x30's were as good as any others, and even better than one of the ten-power models. Mine were brighter and sharper than seven of the eight pair we compared, and just as good as the best pair.

Depending on the bear hunt, spotting scopes can also be useful. When weight is not critical, scopes can help identify a possible bear, or judge a distant bear. When weight is more critical, as in mountain grizzly hunts, scopes are almost mandatory to avoid traveling miles just to identify a possible bear. But in this case, a smaller, compact scope will serve the purpose. As with binoculars, spotting scopes should be waterproof and have quality optics.

*These knee-high rubber boots from Nokia have wool inserts to keep bear hunters warm and dry. The disposable handwarmers can be placed inside the boots each night to dry them out.*

## FOOTWEAR

For coastal brown bear hunting—often inland bear hunting as well—rubber boots are a must. Most of the time this means wearing hip boots. There will be numerous streams and marshy areas in coastal brown bear habitat and these are often negotiated several times in the course of one stalk. There is no time to stop and change from leather hiking boots to hip boots for every crossing.

Many hunters swear by ankle-fit boots because they tend to be easier to walk in. I prefer boot-fit because I hate trying to get out of wet, ankle-fit boots, and I can walk just fine in my boot-fit models. Neither design is great for walking so be sure to bring moleskin or some other blister medicine (Bodyglide slickens the skin to prevent chafing) along for the inevitable hot spots on your feet.

I also have a pair of knee-high rubber boots that often suffice for coastal bear hunts. They have removable felt liners that I change each day. They are made by Nokia (the same company that makes the phones) and come from Finland. They have rigid soles that make walking up, down, and across hills much easier than hip boots with softer soles that roll sidehills.

Some Alaskan bear guides who wear knee-high rubber boots carry a roll of duct tape and rain pants. For crossing deep streams, they will tape the rain pants onto the boots near the ankle and hope no water seeps in while they quickly cross. It works most of the time, but does take extra time. If you are racing to cut off a quickly moving brown bear, this extra time may cost you that bear. But, you may also be able to move faster in good knee-high boots rather than hip boots. In areas with only a few shallow streams and marshes, this knee-high boot and rain pant strategy may work well.

When hunting mountain grizzlies, leather boots may be the best footwear to take. If you are in an area with a low density of bears, and you are covering a lot of higher, drier ground to scout for food sources and bears, leather boots may be the ticket. If you are hunting mountain grizzlies in the spring and there is still plenty of snow and swollen creeks, hip boots may again be the ticket.

On one of my spring, mountain grizzly hunts we wore hip boots because we were hunting up and down a large creek drainage. We found a bear at the 4,000 foot level and had to chase him uphill. We caught him by angling up and across loose scree at a half-run. We just barely managed without twisting an ankle or slipping down the mountainside. In those loose rocks, I wished I had my knee-highs with rigid soles or even hiking boots, but earlier in the day we needed the hip boots to negotiate the creek bottom–so they were the best choice.

One additional advantage of using hip boots is they give off less odor than leather boots–an odor that can alarm bears. Alaska bear hunting terrain is as varied as the state is huge, so the best choice of footwear will be determined by where and when you will hunt.

*Typical hunting clothing that may be suited for field conditions on some Alaskan hunts will not do for bear hunts. This hunter is almost completely covered in waterproof clothing, footwear, and gloves–yet, he is obviously cold and will not do the best job possible when glassing for bears. Bear hunters need special clothing if they are to perform at their highest level.*

## CLOTHING

Water- and wind-proof are also the key words when it comes to choosing clothing for an Alaskan brown bear hunt. You should also dress in layers. Even if you dress in water-proof outer clothing to protect yourself from Alaska's in-cessant, hunting-season rain, you must be able to strip off layers of underclothing when you have to race to cut off a bear. Otherwise, your outer clothing may keep the rain off, but you will get soaked on the inside from your sweat.

Plan ahead each day so you can layer on clothing when you plan to sit for hours while glassing for bears or while in a skiff–cruising a shoreline. By layering, you will be able to strip all but one under-layer off, but still keep on a rain-proof, outer layer if needed, when you have to race a mile or two to cut off that bear of a lifetime.

And, these layers should be synthetic, not cotton. Wool is okay, but not as comfortable near the skin as synthetics, and much heavier and harder to dry out. Bear camps are often cold camps where there is no external heat source to dry wet, wool clothing. Synthetics dry much faster and can be worn while they dry–with minimal discomfort.

There are many good synthetics to choose from. How-ever, bear hunters should choose those brands that claim to reduce odors. Some of the earlier synthetics (polypropy-lene comes to mind) retained odors even after repeated washings. The newer varieties (Powerstretch Polartec for one) claim to reduce odor with antimicrobial action. Since a brown bear's sense of smell is so acute, clothing that re-duces odors is much more preferable for bear hunters.

Alaskan bear-season weather has classic hypothermia temperatures (30-50 degrees) and humidity (100%). Syn-thetic clothing will get you through those times when you will sweat profusely, then get stuck out unexpectedly over-night. Cotton clothing should not be on the list of any Alaskan bear hunter, except for wearing in camp–if you can afford the weight of extra clothing.

One of the most useful items of clothing I take with me on most bear hunts is my Cabela's Waterfowler's Parka. A Waterfowler's Parka is made for wet, windy weather–the typical, coastal bear-hunting weather in Alaska. It is a full-length parka that covers me from my head down to a few inches above my knees. The shell on mine is GORE-TEX, but any good waterproof-yet-breathable layer will do.

It has large pockets with storm flaps for keeping items handy but dry, plus a large storm flap over the main zipper. The roomy hood has wide brims on the sides as well as the top. The hood can be drawn together to form the wide brim into a viewing tunnel to keep out most of the rain and wind, yet still let you see well. The cuffs have Velcro closures to keep out rain, yet are large enough to accommodate the thickest gloves. Finally, it is lined with comfortable, slick nylon and insulated with Thinsulate.

I decided to try one of these coats after noticing most of the seasoned coastal bear guides wore them. They are right; these are great coats for keeping you warm and dry for hours on spotting knobs or while cruising shorelines.

Although your main parka should have a waterproof outer layer, I still suggest carrying another light raincoat for long periods of heavy, driving rain. Mine is a Helly Hansen Impertech raincoat. Like most lightweight coats, it is coated with polyurethane. This makes it waterproof enough for hunting rain gear. The only 100 percent waterproof rain gear is made of rubber. The heavy duty fisherman's rain gear made by Helly Hansen is actually waterproof because it is rubber-coated. If you are cruising in a boat, this might be acceptable. However, this rubber rain gear weighs three times as much as polyurethane-coated models, is much more restrictive, and will become a mobile

*This Waterfowler's coat from Cabela's is just the ticket for bear hunters. It has a GORE-TEX layer, a Thinsulate lining, and both the hood and sleeves close securely to keep out wind and rain. Also pictured are my knee-high boots, their wool liners, my GORE-TEX pants, my synthetic pants, my musher's hat, and my glacier glasses.*

steamroom if you try to hike in it. So it is not practical for bear hunters who will have to walk more than a few hundred yards.

Another item I discovered after observing experienced bear guides is large commercial fishing gloves. The ones I buy are orange and come from a commercial fishing supply store. Mine have a thin lining, and I buy them extra large to fit over synthetic liners. I take two pairs of liners and alternate each day while one pair dries. These are the only gloves or mittens I have found to keep my hands dry and warm all day in driving rain or snow.

If your feet bother you—like mine bother me—in cold weather, you should consider overboots for a bear hunt. These are boots originally designed for treestand hunters to put over their walking boots once they get on their stand. They also work over hip boots to keep your feet warm. I just pack them to my glassing location and put them on there. They are great for long periods of glassing in cold weather, which is typical of brown bear hunting in Alaska.

For long periods of glassing I also take neoprene face masks. The half masks (nose to neck) are great to couple with a full-size balaclava or a large hat, but full-size neoprene masks can also be used. They are amazing at keeping out the cold and rain. You can have every part of your body covered with thick insulation, except for your face between your chin and eyebrows, and still be chilled if the wind is blowing. Covering the rest of your face except your eyes will do an amazing job of warming you up.

If it is really cold and windy, you can go one step further. Wear snowmachine goggles to cover up the last bit of skin on your body. This really makes a difference. By covering all of your skin, you will feel like you are in an enclosed, warm room with no wind or cold affecting you. Of course, goggles can't be used in rainy weather, but they are wonderful when a cold wind is blowing.

As for camouflage while bear hunting, I don't worry too much about getting just the right pattern. Bears don't have the best eyesight, so what I do is take dull colors—or camouflage—that will blend into the dark background. For spring hunting you can take a white suit for crossing snowfields. Lightweight, disposable painter's suits are perfect for this purpose.

On one of my spring guiding hunts, we did not have white suits, but we were creative and succeeded anyway. We had stalked to within 300 yards of a bear that was lying down at the top of a snowfield. We both turned our raincoats inside out so the white linings were exposed and stalked very slowly over the snow. That worked very well as we traveled about 200 yards closer (where we shot from) without the bear noticing us–although he was facing our direction and wide awake.

*Covered from head to foot, including my overboots and goggles, I don't feel any wind and can withstand much colder weather and still remain alert.*

## CAMPING

Camping gear for brown bear hunts is somewhat dependent on where you go. Some camps are placed right next to where your plane lands, some are right on the beach where the boat drops you off, and some are several miles from transportation. How far you are from motorized transportation will determine how elaborate your camp is and how many extras you can bring to make camp life more comfortable. But, as with your other gear, camp gear for bear hunting should be wind- and water-proof.

*To have a comfortable, secure bear camp, start with a proven tent style (like this Bombshelter), stake it down with as many lines as possible, and then surround it with a windbreak (sod is used here).*

Regardless of the size of tent you take on a bear hunt, select one that will withstand strong winds. Whether you are on the coast or in the mountains, winds from 30 to 50 miles per hour are common in Alaska and even stronger winds will occur on occasion. I have personally waited out 80 mile per hour winds one long night while we were deciding whether we should abandon the tent. Although the tent was hidden in 100 yards of ten-foot alders and well-staked, winds strong enough to threaten the tent's very existence still screamed through the brush. That night more than half the camps in the area were damaged–some were exterminated. We were one of the lucky few to escape with only a lack of sleep.

If you are bringing a large, upright tent for comfort, you should consider a "backup" tent. This should be a small, wind-resistant, backpacking tent to be used in case the large tent fails. A good tent seldom fails, unless the conditions are extreme–which they can be during bear hunts.

It is sometimes hard to find a level, flat, protected spot big enough for a large tent, so you compromise and select a less-than-ideal spot. In those situations, it is comforting to know you have a smaller tent you can escape to if your "compromise" location results in a destroyed tent. The small tent can also be used if a bear decides to shred your large tent while you are away hunting one day. Hunting bears has its own set of risks that should be considered when you plan the hunt.

For spring hunts when you might have to camp on snow, a ground cloth to lay under the tent is a good idea. I have often seen two or three feet of snow melt from the beginning of a hunt until the end. All that water has to go somewhere, and I don't like it to go into my tent. A tarp or other waterproof cloth to put under the tent will keep your sleeping quarters much drier. Even if you don't camp on snow, the ground is likely to be wet and/or still frozen, so a ground cloth will still be helpful.

Sleeping cots with pads are always preferable to pads alone if your weight limit allows them. They lift you off the ground in case of a wet floor and provide more space in the tent. Just remember to always fill the void under the cot (with extra gear) to prevent cold air from flowing under your cot, which will unnecessarily rob you of body heat and a good night's sleep. Plus, remember to loop twine around the pad and cot (in two places) so your pad doesn't slide off the cot during the night–and take you with it.

Sleeping bags should be rated to at least ten degrees, and a zero degree rating is better. Bear hunting in Alaska occurs in late fall or early spring. Snow is always possible, as are freezing temperatures for the entire hunt. Since the only difference is a slightly heavier weight for the rating, I always opt for a synthetic bag. The added assurance of warmth, even when wet, makes a synthetic bag a better choice than a down bag–which will be almost worthless when it gets wet.

Rather than taking pillows for comfort, which is very important for hard-hunting bear hunters, you can use an old pillowcase to pack gear inside your duffel. After camp is made, you can stuff extra clothing into the pillowcase for a temporary pillow. An alternative is to use one of those small airline pillows that have synthetic fill and—if needed—wrap it in a soft shirt to bulk it up.

Stove selection depends on the hunt. When weight limits allow them, I take the tried-and-true Coleman two-burner stoves. Either white gas or bottled-gas models work well. Be sure to take plenty of extra gas for either one.

For some Super Cub bear camps (where weight is strictly limited), I take my backpacking stove. I usually take one of my MSR white gas stoves. The bottled-gas stoves would work, but in colder temperatures (below freezing) you may have to warm the bottles before they will function well. The bottled-gas stoves are also more fickle in windy conditions, so they may have to be screened from the wind when cooking outside.

Larger bottled-gas stoves don't usually pose as much of a problem as the one-burner, bottled-gas stoves. They are typically protected from the wind in the vestibule during use, because a larger tent has a large enough vestibule

*This Weatherport is roomy and secure–two important qualities for a
bear camp. The waterproof shipping containers also act as secure
food storage (from camp pests) and seats in camp.*

to cook in, or they are used in a separate cook tent. The fuel
bottles still have to be warm to work well, but larger tents
sometimes have heat sources or have locations (like under
cots wrapped in extra clothing) where bottles can be conve-
niently kept warmer than the outdoor temperature. Just be
careful to keep all fuel (bottled or not) away from direct
heat sources.

A snow shovel or spade can help make any camp more
comfortable. A spade is not as useful for moving snow in
spring, but its utility on hard, frozen ground makes it a better all-around choice. I've dug water trenches around my
tent and countless latrines with spades in bear camps. Shov-
els are bulky and heavy, but very useful items.

Always keep a good gun cleaning kit in bear camp for
obvious reasons. Make sure it is well-supplied with lots of
gun oil or other metal protector. Even stainless or other "rust-
proof" rifles are not corrosion-proof. And coastal bear hunt-

ers will have to deal with salt air as well as water. Either can quickly damage unprotected guns.

## HUNTING

For spring bear hunting, snowshoes are sometimes necessary. It will depend on where you are going, when you are going, and the weather that year. Conditions can vary tremendously between years, so calling ahead to check on local conditions is worth the effort. If there is still deep snow covering most of your hunting area, you may be severely limited to where you can hunt. Deep, soft snow is almost impossible to travel across without some sort of snowshoes.

You will not have to take large trail shoes (the old style), although those do support you well in soft snow. The newer, synthetic models will work just fine, and they are much easier to use through the brushy landscape so typical of bear habitat. The size of shoe you will need depends on your body weight. I am able to use a mid-sized Sherpa snowshoe with aluminum frames and rubber-coated nylon webbing because I weigh only 160 pounds. A 250-pound hunter should take larger shoes with more buoyancy. Since bear hunting often involves climbing steep foothills or real mountains, get the shoes with the traction claws for icy slopes.

Often, snowshoes are only needed during afternoon hikes when the snow softens too much to walk over or for a few short sections where snow hasn't yet melted. Regardless of whether you only need them a few times during the hunt, when you need them, you may really need them. If you are uncertain whether you want to carry five-pound snowshoes when you might never need them, you can just take the very small variety. Even though you may sink in up to your knees, even small shoes will usually make traveling over soft, deep snow possible, whereas without them you may have to abandon a stalk on a real trophy bear. Some very small models that weigh under three pounds are avail-able that may be just the ticket to take in case you need them.

*A snowy April on Kodiak Island typically requires snowshoes if you want to travel above 1,000 feet elevation–but don't forget your rubber boots, you will probably need them, too.*

A large pack with a single compartment (at least 4,000 cubic inches) will work for carrying all your gear for a day and suffice to carry most bear hides. An alternative is to just carry a pack frame (no bag) with a daypack strapped on it. The daypack should be large enough to stuff all your warm clothing into when you have to strip down to a single layer and make a long run to cut off a bear. The daypack can be removed (and carried by your partner), and your trophy bear hide can then be strapped on the pack frame for you to carry back to camp. Any pack bag or daypack should be waterproof, or plastic bags should be carried to protect dry clothing.

I always carry my rangefinder on big game hunts in Alaska. Ravines, low light, excitement, etc., all make range estimation more difficult. A few extra ounces in my pack doesn't make a difference when I'm only a few miles from camp with less than a full pack–typical of bear hunting. My new Bushnell Legend Yardage Pro weighs seven ounces, works out to 800 yards, and is 100 percent waterproof. Although I try to shoot brown bears within 150 yards, I like to be certain of distance because it makes for a more confident shot. Plus, there may be a time when a wounded bear gets out farther than 150 yards, and I will really want my rangefinder if that happens.

For hunting knives, I often bring three on a bear hunt: my three and one-half inch sheath knife (Buck Woodsman), my caping knife (two-bladed Swiss army knife), and a flesher (Outdoor Edge Game Skinner). The sheath knife is for general purpose and most of the skinning, the Swiss army knife is for fine work on the bear's head and feet, and the Game Skinner is for the bulk of the fleshing of the bear hide. Fleshing takes hours, so having a specific tool for fleshing that has several inches of curved blade saves a lot of time and effort.

Unless you are completely familiar with your hunting area, I would suggest taking a GPS. My Garmin Gecko

*At three ounces, this GPS is well worth its weight–considering its
amazing abilities.*

weighs only three ounces and is waterproof. Bear country
can be flat, and it is easy to get disoriented when you are
moving fast and focused on a distant bear. Walking back in
the dark after a chase is also common for bear hunters. A
GPS can make return walks much quicker and safer. I
wouldn't rely 100 percent on a GPS, but for three ounces, it
is worth carrying for the many times it will help.

Another item I would suggest for spring, coastal bear
hunting is a lightweight, winter sled. You can even use the
roll-up sleds (which are easier to pack) with success. This
is the item that can make up for brute strength you don't
have. If no one in the hunting group has enough brute
strength to carry out a huge bear hide, you can drag it on a
sled. The lightweight, winter sleds for kids weigh only a
pound or two and can be left behind much of the time. They
can be packed if a long side trip is taken or fetched from

camp once a large bear is down some distance from camp. They can even be dragged over bare ground for miles before they are unusable. By then the bear will be in camp and the disposable sled has done its work. Sleds should only be taken to bear camps where they will likely be used. This is almost always spring camps near mountains.

For any bear season or camp, it is also possible to make a travois, consisting of two long poles and a tarp between them. Although these were typically pulled by Indian ponies two hundred years ago, bear hunters can pull one of these behind them with the bear hide strapped on it. It is not the greatest invention, but it is as old as the hills and will work in a pinch when the hide is just too heavy to carry on your back (we wish for that kind of success). Some people have also used litters to carry heavy hides, which is just a travois where the dragging end is picked up by another person.

For comfort I take a small, lightweight tarp to wrap up in whenever I get chilled while glassing. Some guides take lightweight stoves or cans of Sterno and cups to make hot liquids to warm up. I always take plenty of disposable handwarmers for warmth. For optimal effectiveness as body-warmers, these should be used on the small of your back, just outside your innermost layer of clothing. The second best place to put these is at the base of the back of your neck, also placed just outside your inner layer of clothing.

With all the talk you hear about rain and wind, it is easy to forget two necessary items: sunblock and lip balm. Fall bear hunting and particularly spring hunting can be nasty, but it can also be nice on occasion. One spring, we set record high temperatures for Cold Bay, Alaska in May. It was 70 degrees and sunny for the entire 15-day spring bear season. Twelve to sixteen hours under the Alaskan sun,

*The Alaskan sun can be brutal on bear hunters during long spring days. This hunter (me) hadn't yet learned to always carry sunblock on any Alaskan hunt, so he had to cover up with gloves and a face mask.*

even in spring, will fry anyone who is not protected. Outfitters were making special flights to drop off sunblock (sun screen was not enough) to their guides and clients. I never hunt in Alaska without a small container of sunblock and a tube of lip balm–with a sunblock component. The sunblock-containing lip balm will save your lips and entire face from chapping in windy weather or burning in sunny weather. It should weigh less than one ounce, but it should always be in your pack.

In my hunting pack I also carry the typical survival and first aid items:  extra knife, compass, matches, lighters, firestarters, space blanket, energy bars, flashlight with spare batteries and bulb, ibuprofen, antibiotics, bandaids, gauze pads, tape, etc.

## TRAVELING WITH GEAR

It is getting more and more complicated and risky to travel to hunting destinations. Restrictions on weight, number of bags, substances, objects, etc. make traveling one of the significant obstacles to a successful hunt. Planning each leg of your trip to avoid delays, damage, and even loss of gear should now be high on the priority list of the traveling hunter.

*Even if you can bring as many bags on commercial jets as you are willing to pay for, you will still be limited by how much you can get into the light plane (like this Super Cub) that takes you to your field camp.*

Airlines have been reducing the number of bags you can carry, and commuter airlines tend to be even more restrictive. Some small Alaskan commuters only allow one bag of 40 pounds or less and charge one dollar or more per pound on the excess—each way. Even the large airlines will charge steep fees ($70 or more) for extra bags over the basic allotment. You should take advantage of the one or two carry-on allowance to reduce your costs and to keep important (but allowable) items under your control. Call ahead for each leg of the trip so you know what to expect, and plan accordingly. It makes sense to pack the fewest bags you can to reduce fees, handling problems, and the chances of losing bags.

Here is a list of important considerations for the traveling hunter:

- •buy good gun or bow cases and add padding to protect your weapons–use extra space to carry soft gear, which will also act as padding;
- •consider buying "take down" weapons so you can use shorter cases that don't look as much like gun cases to would-be saboteurs;
- •always be prepared to open your weapon cases, and realize if you put an external padlock on them, airlines' personnel may cut them off;
- •to insure you will have ammunition, always pack it in the original manufacturer's boxes in each of your checked bags–but not in the gun case;
- •carry cameras in your carry-on to protect them;
- •take double the film you may need, and one or two sets of batteries for the camera and the flash;
- •any film (rolls or in cameras) in a checked bag may be affected by the newer, stronger x-ray machines so don't put these in checked bags;
- •since any film can be affected by walk-through x-ray machines, particularly those in remote places (which describes much of Alaska), take the film out of the canisters, put it in zip-sealed plastic bags, write a description on the bag, and pass it around the x-ray machine;
- •and pack gear and clothing in one- or two-gallon, zip-seal plastic bags for organization and protection from moisture–then use these in field camps for the same purposes.

Another item I always carry with me is a pair of disposable ear plugs. These help me get a good night's sleep in noisy accommodations—like windy nights in a tent, snoring roommates, or noisy hotel rooms. Over-the-counter sleeping pills can also help in these situations or when your sleep schedule is disrupted after traveling over several time zones.

Modern hunters have the resources to prevent many illnesses that would affect their hunt. The main source of illness during remote hunts is the water we drink. It is true that locals build up a resistance to contaminants in the water supply, so you may get sick even when they remain healthy. Although most of the water you may encounter on remote hunts is safe, water filters and treatment tablets are inexpensive and readily available. Even though water tablets (iodine tablets are the most common) and filters are not guaranteed to produce 100 percent safe water unless you use them exactly as directed all the time, for most hunters they are worthwhile insurance against some pretty serious illnesses.

As further "health" insurance, hunters should also pack plenty of mild pain relievers (ibuprofen, aspirin, etc.) in the original containers, antidiarrheals and stomach medicines (Imodium), and extra prescription medication (also in the original containers to minimize security problems). For any Alaskan destination, it may also be worthwhile to ask your doctor to prescribe an array of antibiotics for you to take in case of colds, fever, infections, etc. The more remote your hunt, the more important these precautions become.

After you have painstakingly selected the gear you need and want to take on a hunt, as insurance for your hunt you should pack it well. Don't trust airlines, taxi drivers, or even your outfitter's plane to be gentle with your gear bags. Pad everything so nothing short of a steamroller can damage your hunting gear. Plan ahead, take all the precautions, and your mind will be free to daydream of ten-footers as you begin your brown bear hunt in Alaska.

## BEAR HUNTER'S GEAR CHECKLIST

### CAMPING
__ TENT W/FLY, STAKES,  & ROPES
__ EXTRA TENT
__ GROUND CLOTH
__ TARPS
__ GROUND PAD
__ SLEEPING COT
__ SLEEPING BAG W/LINER, OUTERBAG
__ EXTRA ROPE AND TWINE FOR CAMP
__ AXE, HATCHET & SHARPENING STONE
__ CHAIN SAW, FUEL, OIL & TOOLS
__ SAW, SHOVEL, HAMMER & NAILS
__ CAMP LANTERN, FUEL & SPARE PARTS
__ CANDLE LANTERN &/OR CANDLES
__ WOOD STOVE & WOOD
__ GAS HEATER, FUEL & SPARE PARTS
__ STRIKERS, LIGHTERS & MATCHES
__ FOLDING TABLE & STOOLS
__ PORT-A-POTTI & TOILET PAPER
__ CAMP SHOWER OR SUN SHOWER
__ SMALL RADIO W/SPARE BATTERIES
__ CAMP FLASHLIGHT & ALARM CLOCK
__ CAMP TOOL KIT & FIRST AID KIT
__ INSECT COILS & REPELLANT
__ TAPE & TIE WIRE

### COOKING & EATING
__ CAMP STOVE, FUEL & SPARE PARTS

__ COOK BOX OR STOVE STAND
__ COOKING GRILL
__ COOLER
__ WATER PAIL OR JUG
__ WATER PURIFIER
__ COFFEE POT
__ DUTCH OVEN
__ FRYING PAN, BOILING POTS
__ TWO-QUART DRINKING CONTAINER
__ SPATULA AND LARGE SPOON
__ COOK KNIFE
__ CAN OPENER
__ CUPS AND PLATES
__ TABLESPOONS, FORKS & TEASPOONS
__ ALUMINUM FOIL
__ PAPER TOWELS
__ DISHWASHING TUB
__ POT SCRUBBER/PAD & DISH SOAP
__ PLASTIC TRASH BAGS

### FOOD

(TOO VARIABLE TO LIST, JUST MAKE SURE YOU HAVE EXTRA IN CASE OF WEATHER OR TRANS-PORTATION DELAYS.)

### CLOTHING

__ SOCKS; LINERS & HEAVY DUTY
__ SHORTS & T-SHIRTS
__ LONG UNDERWEAR
__ PANTS & SHIRTS
__ VEST–CAMO &/OR BLAZE ORANGE
__ COAT OR PARKA
__ WIND PANTS AND COAT
__ RAIN GEAR
__ GLOVES, MITTENS & HATS
__ BELT &/OR SUSPENDERS

\_\_ BOOTS, WADERS & CAMP SHOES

\_\_ GAITERS

\_\_ BANDANA

### HUNTING

\_\_ LICENSES, TAGS & REGULATIONS

\_\_ LAND USE PERMIT

\_\_ WEAPONS & AMMO

\_\_ HOLSTER, QUIVER & AMMO POUCH

\_\_ TREESTAND

\_\_ ARMGUARD, TAB, GLOVE & RELEASE

\_\_ GUN, BOW & ARROW CASES

\_\_ CLEANING & REPAIR KIT

\_\_ SPOTTING SCOPE, TRIPOD & BINOS

\_\_ RANGEFINDER

\_\_ GPS/ELT/RADIO

\_\_ FACE NET & CAMO MAKEUP

\_\_ SCENT SHIELD

\_\_ GAME BAGS & PLASTIC BAGS

\_\_ BONE SAW

\_\_ HUNTING KNIVES & SHARPENER

\_\_ DISPOSABLE SURGICAL GLOVES

\_\_ SALT FOR CAPES & HIDES

\_\_ PACK FRAME & BAG

\_\_ DAY &/OR FANNY PACK

\_\_ ROPE, CORD &/OR TWINE

\_\_ MAPS & COMPASS

\_\_ FIRST AID KIT

\_\_ INSECT REPELLANT

\_\_ SPACE BLANKET

\_\_ WATER BOTTLE & SNACKS

\_\_ FLASHLIGHT, EXTRA BATTERIES,  BULB

\_\_ LIGHTER, MATCHES, & FIRESTARTERS

\_\_ CAMERA W/EXTRA FILM & BATTERIES

### PERSONAL

\_\_ TOWEL, WASH RAG & SOAP

\_\_ TOOTHBRUSH, TOOTHPASTE & FLOSS

\_\_ SHAVING KIT & COMB

\_\_ TOILET PAPER & READING MATERIAL

\_\_ PRESCRIPTION MEDICINE
\_\_ EXTRA EYEGLASSES & CONTACTS
\_\_ LIP BALM, ASPIRIN, & ANTACID
\_\_ NEEDLE, THREAD & BUTTONS
\_\_ EXTRA SHOELACES

*This spring-season, Kodiak giant represents what most bear hunters are looking for–huge size (28 8/16 B&C).*

*"It's always helpful to learn from your mistakes, because then your mistakes seem worthwhile."*  –Garry Marshall

# 5
# WHEN & WHERE TO HUNT

*"What you discover on your own is always more exciting than what someone else discovers for you..."*
                                                        –Terrence Rafferty

Of all the big game animals in Alaska, trophy brown and grizzly bears present some of the best opportunities for the average hunter. One reason for this is that a really large, trophy bear can be found just about anywhere in Alaska. It is amazing where some of the really large trophy bears have come from.

One year on Kodiak, locals took two Boone & Crockett brown bears on the road system right near town–with registration permits that anyone could get just for the asking. Within ten miles of my home here in Wasilla, I found nine-foot brown bear tracks just a couple years ago. And moose hunters near here—less than ten miles from downtown—took a Boone & Crockett brown bear just three years ago. Large bears can be found just about anywhere in Alaska by the average hunter with a little initiative.

One of the reasons for this is because bears are so hard to see from airplanes, particularly when they live in forested areas. Large, trophy game animals of many species are often located and then hunted by those with the time and money to fly many scouting hours. But large bears are most often found by hunters on the ground–the average joe hunter. And large bears can be located by average hunters because they leave a track–a track that tells an experienced hunter how large the bear is, right down to the last few inches of hide length.

By looking for food sources that attract bears, average hunters can locate concentrations of un-hunted bears and/ or really large individuals. And since brown or grizzly bears are found in over 90 percent of Alaska, most hunters live within a few miles of these great game animals. Even Anchorage, Alaska's largest city, is currently home to over 60 brown bears according to the Alaska Department of Fish & Game (ADF&G). These bears cannot be hunted in the city, but this just illustrates how capable brown bears are of living within a few miles of human populations–without being noticed by the great majority of the people.

## ALASKA GAME REGULATIONS

Complex is an accurate description of Alaska's game laws. Each year the ADF&G publishes a newly revised edition of the *Alaska Hunting Regulations*. These regulations are valid from July first to June thirtieth of the following year. Everyone hunting in Alaska should obtain a copy of these regulations and read them very carefully–each year they hunt. To avoid breaking game laws, you must know all the current regulations.

Some of the game regulations all bear hunters should know are:

- •nonresidents of Alaska must have a guide or resident relative within the second degree of kindred accompanying them in the field;
- •second degree of kindred means a father, mother, brother, sister, son, daughter, spouse, grandparent, grandchild, brother- or sister-in-law, son- or daughter-in-law, father- or mother-in-law, stepfather, stepmother, stepsister, stepbrother, stepson, or stepdaughter;

*This May brown bear from Chicagof Island, in southeastern Alaska, already has the required locking tag placed on its right foot. Failing to tag an animal immediately after the kill is one of the most common violations in Alaska. This bear squared eight feet, eight inches.*

•brown bear tags are required in most of Alaska, however, there are now several game management units with high bear populations where residents are exempt from the tag requirement;

•where tags are required, they must be locked on the hide immediately after the kill;

•all sport-taken brown bear hides and skulls must be sealed by an official "sealing officer" within a specified time limit–30 days at most;

•in some areas of Alaska, the bear seasons for resident hunters are different than those for nonresident hunters;

•in many areas of Alaska, hunters can only take one brown or grizzly bear every four years, but there are

more and more areas each year with high bear populations where hunters can take one bear every year;
- •evidence of sex must remain naturally attached to all brown bear hides;
- •a brown or grizzly bear cub is defined as a bear in its first or second year of life–cubs are not legal bears;
- •hunters cannot hunt or kill brown bears within one-half mile of a garbage dump or landfill;
- •and snowmachines can be used to hunt brown bears, but they cannot be used to chase them, nor can hunters shoot from the machines.

Most nonresidents choose to hire an Alaskan guide when hunting brown bears, because they do not have a resident relative within the second degree of kindred who has the desire—or ability—to accompany them on a brown bear hunt. Sitting in a field camp does not qualify as "accompanying." To meet this requirement, a resident relative must actually "accompany during each day's hunt" the nonresident hunter.

Brown bear hunts are some of the most expensive hunts in the state, ranging from as little as $6,000 for some Interior grizzly hunts to as much as $15,000 for Kodiak or Alaska Peninsula brown bear hunts. Hunters looking for a guide can contact the state's Division of Occupational Licensing for a list of all Alaskan registered guides.

## BEAR HUNTING SEASONS

Alaska's 365,000,000 acres are divided into 26 game management units (GMU's). Twenty four of these GMU's have brown bear seasons. The open seasons in these 24 GMU's vary from 16 days a year to 365 days a year. In some units, the season dates even vary from year to year.

In general, there are fall and spring brown bear seasons. September and October are typical fall seasons; April

*One major concern for spring bear hunters is rubbed hides. This Spring Kodiak bruin had a good hide and just made the B&C minimum at 28 0/16.*

and May are typical spring seasons. In GMU 13, there is such a large and growing bear population, there is now no closed season on brown bears. In this GMU, plus several others in the state, there is also a bag limit of one bear every year and residents are exempt from the bear tag requirement. Of all big game populations in Alaska, brown bears are probably the healthiest, with seasons becoming more and more liberal over the past decade or two.

In the two areas that produce the largest bears—Kodiak Island and the Alaska Peninsula—hunting seasons are under tighter controls to prevent overharvest. Most of the bear hunting on Kodiak is regulated by a drawing-only system, although guides are automatically allotted a fixed number of permits for their clients without going through the drawing system. Rather than control the harvest on the Alaska Peninsula with another drawing system, the ADF&G uses alternating, short spring and fall seasons. In odd-numbered years, there is a three-week fall season; in even-numbered years, there is a two-week spring season. In this way, anybody can hunt there without having to win a drawing permit, but the short, open seasons limit the harvest. The bear populations on both Kodiak and the Peninsula are large and stable or growing, so both management systems are working well.

In addition to Kodiak Island, there are several other drawing permit areas for brown bears. There are both spring (May 1-31) and fall (Nov. 1-Dec. 6) application periods for certain hunts. Hunters must apply during the specified application period for each hunt to qualify.

There are also several GMU's where harvest is controlled with registration permits. Registration permits give game managers more control over the legal harvest. Any legal hunter can sign up for a registration hunt, but strict reporting requirements allow game managers to close seasons prematurely if a predetermined number of bears are taken.

A few remote areas of Alaska even have subsistence brown bear hunting seasons. These are restricted to area residents, the meat must be salvaged for human consumption, and ADF&G takes the front claws and skin of the head—eliminating the trophy aspect of the bear.

Bowhunters pursuing brown bears in Alaska can hunt any open seasons. There are a few equipment requirements for hunting brown bears with a bow (see Chapter 11, "Bowhunting Bears"), but if these are met, bowhunters are included in the general category of hunters for open seasons, registration permits, and drawing permits.

## TROPHY QUALITY

The season—spring or fall—you choose to hunt brown bears will affect the quality of your trophy, the number of

*One of the most commonly rubbed areas on spring bears are their feet. This Kodiak bear has plenty of hair on its feet and will make a great rug or life-size mount.*

bears you will see, and how you will hunt them. The timing of your hunt within each season will affect your hunt in the same ways, but in a subtler manner. Here is a chart comparing several factors of a bear hunt depending on the season.

# SPRING   OR   FALL?

| | | |
|---|---|---|
| **WEATHER:** | poor to great | poor to great |
| **HIDES:** | poor to great | usually **good** |
| **NUMBERS:** | low to high | medium to **high** |
| **VISIBILITY:** | **best** | poor to good |
| **ALERTNESS:** | **low** to high | medium to high |
| **SPEED:** | **slow** to fast | slow to fast |
| **NOCTURNAL:** | **some** | many |

Alaskan weather in spring and fall can vary from cold, wet, and windy to sunny and warm. You should be prepared to hunt during any type of weather by having the proper gear.

The quality of hides on the bears you will see can vary greatly. Spring hides can have long, dense, luxurious hair–the most beautiful trophies you could hope for. They can also be rubbed to the point that any hunter will pass on the bear. To some extent, you will see better hides the earlier you go in the spring. However, in some years almost all the bears will already have a few rubbed spots when they come out of their dens. But, the earlier you go, the fewer bears you are likely to see, so your choices may be limited.

Fall bear hides are not as likely to be poor; the lower limit is generally just okay. But the upper limit in quality of fall bear hides is only good, not great like spring when the bears still have their winter coat of hair. Overall, fall bear hides have a slight edge in average quality over spring bear hides.

*Fall bear hides are more predictably good than spring hides. This large Alaskan Peninsula brownie had a good hide, but not a great hide. Spring hides can be great if they haven't rubbed any of their four to six-inch hair off–either in the den or after they emerge (28 8/16 B&C).*

During spring bear hunts, you never know how many bears you will see. Each year is different because of the timing of spring weather and the amount of snowfall left from winter. The number of bears can range from very low to high. In fall, the number of bears is much more constant for each area. In areas where there are strong salmon runs (the most common food that concentrates bears in the fall), you are almost guaranteed to see similar numbers of bears from year to year in a given area. There are rare occasions when the salmon run crashes in an area and the bears are not concentrated as in normal years, but the bears are still in the general area and moving a lot in search of food. In areas without salmon runs to attract bears, the number of bear sightings in fall is usually pretty constant because un-like spring, all the bears are out feeding–you just have to locate them. Because bear numbers are more predictable in fall, this season is a slightly better choice in this category.

Visibility of bears, both over distance and for spotting tracks in the snow, is much better in spring than fall. Bears can be seen for up to five miles—or more with good optics—on snowfields and then intercepted. In fall, the leaves and brush make visibility much poorer, and since spotting bears is half the battle, spring is a much better choice in this category.

In spring, brown bears are much less alert than in the fall. Spring bear hunters often spot bears that obviously just came out of the den. Bears will walk slowly, lie down and rest often, and just look "sleepy." Stalking these bears is much easier because of their lack of awareness. Spring is a much better time to get up on a bear—particularly the big ones—because of this.

Both spring and fall bears range in speed from slow to fast. At times, bears in both seasons will be moving at a constant walk, which is generally faster than hunters can walk. There are also situations when bears are feeding in one spot or moving slowly, and these bears can be caught by fast-walking hunters. But there tend to be more slow-moving, spring bears because they just came out of the den or they are searching for food. Because of this, spring bear hunting produces more opportunities from slow-moving bears. On many of my spring hunts, the only reason we were able to intercept a bear was the fact it had to lie down to rest periodically. In fall, these same bears would have outwalked us easily.

The last factor to consider when deciding which season to hunt is the nocturnal habits of the bears. Spring bear season is the hands-down choice for hunters. Spring bears are typically active anytime of the day–regardless of their

*When hunting coastal areas in the spring, many of the landings will be on the smooth beaches at low tide, as these hunters have done.*

size. Fall bears—particularly the larger trophies—are often only seen at dawn and dusk, preferring to feed under cover of darkness and the safety it offers. Some of the really old, wise, and large bears won't even be seen during any daylight hours. Based on their nocturnal habits, spring bear season is better than fall season for really large bears.

Deciding whether to hunt spring or fall should be based on these factors as well as on the hunter. If a long-haired spring hide is of paramount importance, then choose spring. If you just want the best chances at one bear, choose late spring for most areas. If you are a bowhunter, or can't walk much and want to sit and wait by a salmon stream, choose fall. If you want the best chance at a large bear, choose spring. For the average rifle hunter, I would recommend going in the spring for most areas. You also have to consider the area you are hunting and if you want to hunt anything else in the same time frame. The season you choose should be based on all the factors that are important to you.

*Brown bears from the inland areas of Alaska tend to be smaller, on average, than Kodiak and Alaskan Peninsula bears. This Mulchatna bear is classified as a brown bear by Boone & Crockett and a grizzly by SCI. Either way, it still represents a great experience, and an outstanding trophy for the lucky hunter.*

## PLACES TO HUNT

With over 300,000,000 acres to hunt brown bears in Alaska, it can be difficult to choose your hunting area. If you are just after any brown bear, or you know exactly what you are looking for in a trophy, then the task is much easier. Once you establish your basic requirements, you need to learn the general population densities, the population characteristics, and the hunting styles used in each area of the state.

Kodiak Island, the Alaska Peninsula, and southeastern Alaska are the most popular areas–mostly because they produce the largest bears in good numbers. They are also the most costly to hunt, with guides charging $10,000 to $15,000 per client.

Kodiak Island bear hunting is mostly limited to drawing permits, although there is an area near the town of Kodiak that is managed with registration permits. The annual harvest on Kodiak is about 160 bears* (see note one at the end of this chapter). The average age of the harvested bears is about seven years and their skull size is about 24 inches. Over half of the largest one hundred brown bears in the Tenth Edition of the Boone & Crockett record book came from Kodiak Island. Hunters who are looking for a really large brown bear should consider Kodiak Island** ( see note two at the end of this chapter).

The Alaska Peninsula brown bear harvest is about 320 bears per year. The average age of the harvested bears is about seven years. The average skull size of the harvested bears is 23 inches–about one inch smaller than those on Kodiak. Although there is only one spring or one fall season open each year (spring and fall seasons aren't open in the same year), any eligible hunter can hunt the Alaska Peninsula without having to first win a drawing permit. This makes the Peninsula another attractive choice for many hunters who want a large bear.

Brown bears harvested from the Alaska Peninsula number just slightly less than those from Kodiak Island in the Boone & Crockett record book. However, since the harvest on the Peninsula is twice as high as that on Kodiak, the percentage of harvested bears that are really large is much higher on Kodiak.

However, the Peninsula does attract a high number of both resident and nonresident hunters. The first year I hunted there in the fall bear season, there were so many gun shots echoing over the grass flats, it sounded like the opening day of duck season. Since the seasons are compressed into two or three weeks, there can be a lot of pressure in a short time span. I regularly hear stories about conflicts between bear hunters on the Peninsula. Because of this, hunters opting for an Alaska Peninsula bear hunt need to search out specific areas where there will be room for them to hunt without intruding on nearby camps.

Beyond the Alaska Peninsula lies Unimak Island–a bear haven. Brown bear hunting is controlled by drawing permits–just like on Kodiak Island. An average of 11 bears are taken each year, and they average over eight years old. Their skull size averages over 25 inches–the largest average of any area. However, the number of permits is very small and the odds of drawing one are very low. The remote location of the island also makes it one of the most expensive brown bear hunts in Alaska.

Game management units one, four, five, and six include Alaska's coastal brown bear habitat from the tip of southeastern Alaska to, and including, Prince William Sound. This area produces about 250 brown bears per year. The harvested bears average about six and one-half years in age, and their skull size averages about 22 inches. The price for a guided hunt in this large area is lower than either Kodiak Island or the Alaska Peninsula, but the average size of the bears is slightly smaller.

These three, southern coastal areas—Kodiak Island, the Alaska Peninsula (including Unimak), and southeast-

*No matter where you hunt brown or grizzly bears in Alaska, hunter satisfaction is often more a frame of mind than a result of the size of the bear. This hunter's smile tells everything about his satisfaction with his hunt. This Kodiak scored 27 8/16 B&C.*

ern Alaska through Prince William Sound—produce about 750 brown bears per year for hunters. The remaining brown bear (not grizzly) areas of Alaska produce another 350 bears per year. These remaining areas (see map, Chapter Two, page 24) produce an occasional Boone & Crockett bear, but these brown bears are noticeably smaller on average. Of course, in any of these areas, the hunter's ability to spot bears, judge their size, and then hold out for a large one can be as important as the area's average bear size in determining what size of trophy a particular hunter takes home.

However, size is not the only criterion for judging bear trophies. Bear hunters can still take home some great trophies from the inland areas of Alaska that hold good populations of brown bears. Additionally, many of these areas are also less costly to hunt–for both residents and nonresidents. Most hunters would be happy to take home an eight- or nine-foot brown bear, and there is always the chance to bag one of those occasional ten-footers, since they can be found throughout Alaska brown bear range.

For hunters after a large bear recognized by the one of the record books as a grizzly, there is one inescapable fact: Canada produces most of the large grizzlies. Almost 70 of the top 100 grizzlies in the Boone & Crockett record book come from Canada–mostly British Columbia (B.C.). The reason for this is simply because the boundary line allows for coastal brown/grizzly bears in B.C. to be entered as grizzlies.

The portion of the boundary line that follows the Alaskan Panhandle border between Canada and Alaska is very close to the coast and even right on the coast in places. All the bears in Canada thus become grizzlies, even though they are very near the coast and have access to a higher protein food supply that few grizzly bears in Alaska get. These British Columbia grizzlies also live at a more southern latitude than any Alaskan grizzlies, so their denning time is shorter and they have a much longer growing season. However, Alaska does produce about 30 percent of the record book grizzlies, so we do have plenty of large bears.

As is the case with coastal brown bears, the near-coast grizzly bears often get larger because they enjoy a diet rich in high-protein salmon. Hunters mainly concerned with size can hunt the coastal areas of Alaska north of the grizzly boundary line, the 62nd parallel of latitude.

Wherever grizzlies are found in Alaska, there is a chance of finding a large animal. All grizzly populations have the genetic ability to produce large animals if a bountiful, high-protein diet is available. I've seen really large grizzlies hundreds of miles inland on the North Slope of the Brooks Range–classic grizzly habitat with a limited food supply, a short growing season, and resulting low bear densities. I believe the largest grizzlies just learn to exploit

*Once large boars surpass most of the other bears in size, they not only get the best fishing spots, they also may become efficient predators on moose and caribou. Having access to both of these rich sources of protein (fish and large ungulates) makes it possible for them to grow to an exceptional size, like this Kodiak bruiser.*

moose (and maybe caribou) more fully than the smaller bears, which also results in a longer growing season. Once these bears get large enough and smart enough they can actually take down adult moose. This ability to periodically get huge amounts of high-protein food and delay their denning into late October because they can still find plenty of food, makes for some really large bears.

I'm basing this observation—in part—on an early October moose and caribou hunt I took to the North Slope of the Brooks Range. We saw several large grizzlies either hunting or eating adult moose. In one case, a large bull moose had walked out into the middle of a river to avoid a huge grizzly. The water depth was deep enough the grizzly had to swim so he was ineffective as a predator. The moose— with its longer legs—was able to stand in the river and the grizzly had to give up and swim back to shore.

Another large bear we saw had just taken an adult moose, and this bear was every bit of nine feet and maybe more. We actually walked within 100 yards of this bear when he false-charged us to keep us away from his kill. He was large enough to drag the entire moose over 50 yards, across an eight-foot-deep stream, and then deep into an alder patch. It is this type of bear that finally gets large enough to kill adult moose, which can then grow to huge proportions because of this new source of rich protein. Only a few bears (if any) in an area may get to this point in size and ability, so hunters may have to search extensively for them. In an area like the North Slope, where bear densities can be less than one bear per 100 square miles, this search, to be successful, may have to cover a lot of ground.

*This large boar was spotted at high noon one spring day, just walking around looking for food. Spring season bears—even the large boars—are often not as alert as they should be. Whether it is their hunger or because they are still not fully awake, they are much easier to find and to stalk in spring than in fall.*

Wherever you hunt coastal brown bears or grizzly bears in Alaska, there is always the chance you may find a really large bear. The key factor in how large a bear gets is the amount of food it eats. On one of my Kodiak deer hunts, we were several days into the hunt before we noticed large bear tracks in the area. Upon further investigation, we discovered the ten-foot-class Kodiak bear was cleaning up our gut piles at night. We never saw the bear in daylight, nor did it ever come into our camp where several deer were hanging within easy reach. It was wise enough to stay away from us dangerous humans, and wait until the safety of darkness to sniff out our deer kill sites for what we left behind. This is exactly how a bear can get really large in a fairly accessible spot—we were only a few miles from a large village.

In another instance, I was hunting moose in an area within earshot of an Alaskan suburb. Tracks of a nine-foot brownie told a story of a bear cleaning up moose gut piles—perhaps also under the cover of darkness. We guessed this bear had learned to capitalize on this regular, rich, fall food source (moose entrails, bones, and hides), but also learned to stay out of sight to survive. I may still go after this bear if I can figure out how to catch him in the daylight.

Since most hunters are looking for large boars, they need to be aware of those areas that attract mainly sows with cubs. These areas usually have a good source of high quality food (salmon or berries are the most common) plus plenty of nearby cover. If the area also has hunting pressure, this will also tend to drive away the older, wiser boars more than the sows. The best indicators that you have found one of these areas are: there are no large, single tracks and you are seeing all sows and cubs and/or immature boars. It is best to find another hunting area in these situations.

Brown bear hunting in Alaska presents great opportunities for high success rates and large trophies. Bear populations are healthy and growing virtually throughout Alaska. Average resident hunters with minimal financial investments can have great hunting both in terms of numbers of bears and size of trophies, and can find these opportunities relatively close to home. Nonresident hunters—although their cost may be considerably higher—also have these same opportunities for great brown bear hunting. Unlike any other big game hunting in Alaska, brown bear hunting is about as good as it's ever been, and the vast majority of bear populations are growing!

*"A window of opportunity won't open itself."* –Dave Weinbaum

*The harvest data for my statements in this chapter came courtesy of the Alaska Department of Fish & Game. I was given raw data and based the statements on my own analyses of the data.

**Success rates for brown bear hunters are not available because the ADF&G does not require hunter reports except from successful hunters, registration permit hunters, and those hunters who had drawing permits.

# 6
# CAMPING IN BEAR COUNTRY

*"There is always a best way of doing things (even) if it be boil an egg."* –Ralph Waldo Emerson

A good bear camp will serve two purposes: it will make you comfortable, and it will improve (or at least not hinder) your chances of success. Your camp will achieve these two goals if you choose a good general camp location within your hunt area, select the right spot for your tent, and then pitch the tent in the best manner possible.

One of my recent open-tundra camps is a good example. We wanted to stay near the airstrip for convenience, to minimize our scent trails, and because bears were distributed evenly in the entire area. We didn't need to travel anywhere to improve our odds of success. The open tundra didn't offer much protection from the inevitable windstorms, except for one large depression made by the same piece of equipment that made our airstrip many years prior to the hunt. So, we placed the tent in the depression and staked it well from every corner and from all the other tie-downs. We also re-tied it after a couple days to remove any slack that had developed.

The one worry we had was water accumulating in our "hole" if we had a lot of rain. To allow for that, we placed a floor-sized tarp down under the tent and dug trenches around its perimeter. The inevitable strong windstorms came and blew harmlessly over the top of the tent. The heavy rains came, were caught in our trenches, and we stayed dry. We were comfortable, slept well, and our minds were free to focus on hunting, and not the weaknesses of our tundra home.

## WHERE TO CAMP

The decision of where to camp within your hunting area is sometimes simple. If you know the area you are hunting, there may be obvious locations to camp. Sometimes there is realistically only one place to camp because of transportation limitations (the only strip or lake in the area) or a severely limited hunting area.

Many bear hunting areas have a fairly even distribution of bears or, at least, an even distribution of bear hot spots accessible from any one spot. Since one of the rules of bear hunting is to minimize your scent trails, bear camps are often located very near to where your mechanized transportation ends. It is often best to camp right there and not hike through bear habitat–leaving a scent trail that will spook bears completely out of the area. Since it is also true that bears (in many areas) are as likely to walk right by camp as they are to walk at some distance from camp, there is often no reason to hike to establish camp.

I learned this lesson early in my bear-guiding career. One of the most difficult aspects of brown bear hunting for first-time hunters is to stay put and spend your time looking. I succumbed to one of my first client's wishes on day four of his hunt, so we left camp in search of a bear. We took a decent mountain grizzly that afternoon a few miles from camp. From day one of the hunt, I had tried to convince him of the prudence of just staying put and searching with our binoculars, rather than leaving scent trails everywhere as we searched with our hiking legs. I promised him that if we stayed put, we would have a good bear walk right by camp within five days. As we sat in camp fleshing his bear on day five, a nice grizzly walked within 150 yards of us. He got some great video footage to take home, plus he was then convinced I was the epitome of Alaskan guides because I had predicted that bear on day five.

*Even when your tent can be placed next to high bushes or trees that provide a windblock, always use as many guy line tie downs as are provided. You will sleep better and be more convinced your tent will still be there after you return from a hard day of bear hunting.*

When you do have a choice of where to place your camp within your selected area, there are several factors to consider. If bears are concentrated on a salmon-filled stream, a hillside covered with a bumper crop of berries, or a beach with plenty of bear food, you will want to be close enough to hunt those bears–but not so close your camp spooks them. Here are the other factors I use to decide where to establish a bear camp:

  •camp downwind of any major feeding area when possible–beaches, ravines, and drainages often have prevailing winds that can sometimes be used to your advantage for camp placement;

- place camp where any daily walk you take to get to a good viewing area will have a prevailing wind that doesn't contaminate the most productive area;
- camp within walking distance of a good spotting knob that gives you a view of most of the good feeding areas, travel routes, or simply lots of bear habitat;
- have a good view of bear habitat right from camp–if possible;
- try to camp near a natural windbreak;
- try not to camp right on waterways on which bears often travel;
- and try to choose a camping area that has suitable locations for a tent.

You will not always be able to satisfy all of these criteria, but the better you are at selecting the most suitable area to camp, the better your hunt is likely to be.

*Selecting a spotting knob close to camp will allow you to not only keep your human scent trails to a minimum, but may also permit you to sneak back to camp for a mid-day siesta. This spring season bear hunter will have over sixteen hours of good glassing light, which is a long time to remain fully alert in the warm, spring sun.*

# PITCHING CAMP

Once you have chosen the general area for camp, there are many factors to consider when you set up your camp. Picking the exact spot for the tent and then pitching it properly can make a huge difference in your comfort, and maybe your hunting success. If your tent threatens to blow down every night, or it continually flaps all night long, or you just don't trust it to be there when you return from a day-long hunt, you will not hunt as efficiently as you could.

When choosing the tent location you should look for (in this order of importance) a dry, wind-protected, level, flat spot that is not on or near a game trail, and has a good view of your hunting area. The first four of these criteria can be altered to some extent. A slightly damp spot can be covered with a waterproof groundcloth and work out just fine. You can also gather dry vegetation to build up an area before placing a tent (with or without a groundcloth) on it. Dry vegetation can also be used to level an area or to smooth a bumpy spot.

If no natural wind protection exists, windbreaks can be added. On open tundra, you can cut large blocks of tundra (if it is permissible in the area) and stack them on the windward side of the tent. Just 18 inches of wind-block makes a huge difference because the short wall slows the wind and directs it upward. The slower, upward-directed wind has a lot less effect on a tent than if it were full-strength. Blocks of snow can be used in the same way on spring hunts.

If there are any brush patches at all, they should be fully utilized for wind protection. Alder patches make some of the most comfortable tent locations available. By just cutting as few as a half-dozen alders, you can usually create a dry, level, flat tent spot with great wind protection for large tents.

If high winds are a possibility—and most of Alaska meets this criterion—I first find the leeward side of a large alder patch. Then, I cut a narrow, ten-foot long path into the brush patch, turn 90 degrees, and cut another five feet. Next, I remove the alders from a spot slightly larger than my tent at the end of the path. Placing the tent inside the alder patch makes a much quieter, safer place to stay for the duration of the hunt. Plus, the alders make great tie-off anchors for the tent. Stake down the bottom securely, then tie your tent's upper tie-off rings to the base of alders. On windy days or nights, the alder tie-offs will give just a little and allow the tent to flex slightly–making it much sturdier and more likely to stay erect.

**<u>Figure 6A</u>**

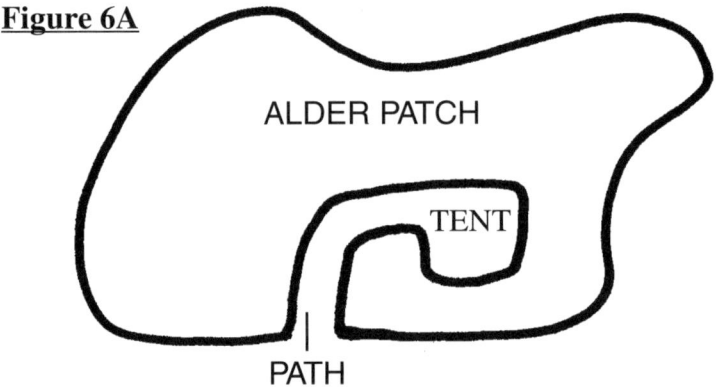

*Using this type of design for placing a tent will help reduce the wind reaching the tent and make for a more comfortable camp, as long as the local land regulations allow for cutting a little brush.*

I also use the flexing nature of alders when I put a tarp over the tent vestibule or, when it is too windy a location for that, to make a covered, outside cooking/eating area. If I have a fairly well-sheltered tent location inside an alder patch, I will tie a large tarp over the tent and let it overhang the door by about ten feet. I leave the alders intact and just drape the tarp over the alders, tying down the tarp's corners and edges close to the ground so wind can't get underneath them. Next, I get underneath the tarp and cut only what is needed to have space to sit, cook, and eat. The tops of the alders will prop the tarp up like a tent and let it give with the wind–which makes it much less susceptible to being blown down or tearing.

In places where the tent may get too much wind for this arrangement, I make a similarly constructed, tarped area within an alder patch separate from the tent. I usually make it just tall enough to sit up on a chair. Any taller, and it would be much more likely to get destroyed in a windstorm.

I use these tarped areas because I try to avoid cooking in the tent, but I don't want to cook in the rain. Many hunters do cook inside their tents, but they have to be sure to leave the door(s) open to avoid carbon monoxide poisoning–a tragedy which happens to campers every year. They also have to be very careful not to burn down their tent and/or their gear.

To make a good, sturdy, tarped vestibule, bring lots of small rope or heavy twine to tie the tarp down from as many points as possible. Sometimes these tarped areas can be put on slight hillsides within a few feet of the tent, but protected from most of the strong winds. Since tents require drier and leveler ground, they often cannot be placed in these types of protected spots where you can put your tarped, cooking area.

Some additional considerations for making and maintaining a comfortable, successful bear camp are:
- whenever possible, point a corner and/or the lowest side of the tent at the prevailing wind–avoid facing high, flat tent sides directly into the wind;
- taller tents are more comfortable, but also more susceptible to strong winds–choose your tent to fit your hunting location and your ability to pitch the tent;
- don't pitch your tent in the path of running water–from rain accumulation or from melting snow;

•use long, sturdy stakes to hold your tent–alder branches are great for this;

•use deadman anchors when the ground is not solid or you are camping on snow;

•tighten your tent tie-downs after every windy day, every windy night (before you walk away in the morning), and even in the middle of very windy nights;

•tie off to all possible points on your tent;

•dig a latrine downwind of the tent and drop a shovel of dirt down it every time to reduce odors;

•always keep your extra, dry clothes in plastic bags (two gallon zip-seals or garbage bags) inside the tent just in case (of whatever might happen in a hunting camp);

•don't spend unnecessary time or leave unnecessary odors near shorelines that bears may visit;

•and avoid placing your tent on hilltops, in the centers or at the lower ends of ravines, or any place that looks like a wind funnel–sit for a few minutes and think of the possibilities before plopping down your tent.

## EATING

Cooking and food odors from your camp can affect your bear hunting success. Although food odors may attract some bears, they are not usually the trophy bears you are after. Trophy bears are more likely to run away when they smell anything that means humans are near.

If you have a bear camp more than a mile away from any likely bear habitat on wide-open, hilly tundra with strong winds, you may only have to take a few precautions when cooking or eating. However, if you are a bowhunter, or will sit on a stand, or have to camp close to a concentrated food source or a heavily used travel route, or are hunting in an area where bears are habituated to humans (mainly our food

*Young, cute bears like this one are often the most troublesome camp
bears because they are not very skilled at finding food, (therefore,
they are often hungry) and they haven't yet learned to fear humans.*

and garbage), you should take a few more precautions about
your cooking and eating habits during your bear hunt.

Normal precautions for any bear camp include keeping a clean camp, always putting any garbage into plastic
bags immediately, keeping food inside tight containers, and
disposing of dishwater and cooking water at least 100 feet
away from camp. Most of these precautions will help prevent any problem bears (or other camp pests) from coming
into camp. Most problem bears are young (small) or sows
with older cubs. Assuming you do not want to shoot any of
these types of bears, it pays to eliminate anything that will
attract them–i.e., food/garbage odors.

Bowhunters or hunters who will sit on a stand should
remove their hunting clothes while in camp. Both types of
hunters may get very close to bears for a long time and
should take all precautions they can to eliminate odors—

with scent-blocking clothes and sprays—and not add to the problem by bringing human cooking odors into the field with them.

Some hunting situations require you to camp close to the bears you will hunt. These may require you to:

•have a cold camp (no cooking);

•cook one-pot meals to reduce odors and clean-up remnants;

•choose drier, less pungent food;

•place all your food in bear-proof containers, and/or hang it out of reach of bears;

•and be extra careful to avoid fuel spills–bears are attracted to the smell of diesel and kerosene.

If you are hunting around bears that are habituated to humans, there may well be "camp bears" around that are looking for human food or garbage. Once a "camp bear" finds yours, it will keep coming back until all your food is gone, you are gone, or you have to kill it. Taking precautions will not only save you trouble in camp, or perhaps save your hunt altogether, it may also save a bear's life for a future hunting opportunity.

Camping skills can be an important factor in your bear hunting comfort and success. This is partly because of the problems a nuisance brown bear can cause in a camp and partly because of the nasty weather so prevalent during Alaska's brown bear seasons. Learning to be an expert camper can be an achievement in itself. Regardless of the trophies you do or do not bring home, being an expert camper can guarantee that you will enjoy every hunt you take in Alaska–and that is a worthwhile achievement.

*"Out there where the forest brushes the sky, that's my kind of country."* –Louis L'Amour

# 7
# HUNTING BEARS

*"Opportunity dances with those already on the floor."*
–H. Jackson Brown, Jr.

The majority of brown bear hunting in Alaska is spot and stalk hunting. Other successful hunting methods are cruising along shorelines or floating rivers to locate bears, waiting on a stand near a food source or travel route, or using snowmobiles to search for bears. The method you choose will depend on the location of the hunt, the time of year, the density of bears in the area, the distance you can shoot accurately, the amount of time you have for the hunt, and your personal preference of hunting style. Whichever method you choose, remember to allow extra time in case you encounter a stretch of Alaska's notoriously foul weather.

Brown bears are perhaps the most unpredictable of all big game animals in Alaska. There are, of course, many predictable aspects of bear behavior, but brown bears are liable to feed, fight, or play at any time of day or night, and at any location they happen to be. When you add mating activity during the spring season, this adds up to a very interesting and educational hunt each time you hunt bears.

Because brown bears have so many behavior patterns, regardless of how many times a person hunts bears, there will always be more to learn. The best hunters are those that keep an open mind to learning more behavior patterns. There will be times when you will make an observation, and then remember one or more past observations, and then have one of those "aha!" moments, when you put two and two together. Suddenly a bear's behavior makes sense, and you have identified a pattern that you can use in the future to anticipate what a bear will do.

These "aha!" revelations are vital lessons for every serious bear hunter because no matter how complete a book is—even this one—there are too many brown bear behavior patterns for any hunter, or group of hunters, to have encountered every one. Plus, bears are very adaptive and continually alter their behavior patterns to out-compete other bears and to simply survive. This chapter describes dozens of bear behaviors I've gleaned from four decades of personal experience, conversations with other bear guides and hunters, and volumes of books and magazines about bears. Just remember these behaviors are not the end-all, but they are a good starting point.

## SPOTTING BEARS

Brown bears are large omnivores that require a lot of calories to sustain themselves. However, the ratio of calories produced per square mile in Alaska is generally low. The two results of these facts are: brown bear population densities are quite low, and each bear typically travels many miles each day in search of food. Because brown bears are usually moving during much of their waking time, spot and stalk hunting is the most successful method of hunting.

Most bear hunters prefer to remain stationary while glassing for bears, as opposed to hiking and looking. There are three reasons for this: 1) bears are short animals that blend in well so they are often difficult to spot; 2) moving hunters will miss bears that stationary hunters will often spot; and 3) hiking through bear habitat spreads human scent that will spook bears out of the hunting area.

*Brown bears can be very difficult to spot because their coloration matches much of their habitat, and because they are short animals. This mountain brown bear slipped by us while we took a five-minute nap, but we woke in time to see him walking away and still caught him before he escaped over a mountain pass.*

I've read that brown bears can smell a human's tracks up to 48 hours after they are made. I can't verify that by personal experience, but I have seen several examples of how good their sense of smell is. During one of my Kodiak hunts, after walking upstream for two hours in rubber boots, we spotted a large boar coming toward us. We hunkered down in the shoreline brush and waited–the hunter with his bow and I with the backup rifle.

The bear had almost crossed the twenty-foot stream right in front of us when he jerked to a stop. His nose had smelled our boot tracks on the stream bank from 15 feet, even though he was coming directly downwind. There must have been a slight swirl in the wind, and his keen nose picked up what little scent had come off our washed, rubber boots and settled on the bank. In an instant, the boar whirled, bounded out of the stream, and ran full speed back the way he came–even though he never spotted us. As he galloped away, he acted like a whipped dog–looking back over his shoulder in our direction, trying to catch a glimpse of the animals he feared most–humans.

*The more details hunters pay attention to, the more likely they are to bag bears like these two ten-footers. Scent is one of those details bear hunters must always have foremost in their minds.*

One of the first and most important tasks when establishing (most) bear camps is to find a suitable spotting knob. The main criteria to look for when choosing a spotting knob are close proximity to camp, favorable wind direction, and a commanding view. A commanding view of the best bear feeding areas or travel routes is the number one feature of a good spotting knob. In many areas, there are no geographical features like main rivers, shorelines, or main bear trails to concentrate bears. Also, bears tend to travel through their habitat without much regard to geographical features, like most species do. So a "commanding view" often just means being able to see as much ground as possible.

The shorter distance you have to walk each day to reach your spotting knob, the less you will spread your scent over the area. Also, since dawn and dusk are the best times to look for bears, a longer distance often results in using flashlights. The light is more likely to disturb bears that you don't even see in the darkness. Walking in the dark through bear country is also a little more dangerous, because bears tend to be more aggressive in the dark, particularly the young, foolish bears that are less desirable as trophies.

Another advantage of having a nearby spotting knob is to make returning to camp for a midday nap more convenient. For short naps, I often just curl up in a nearby alder patch. One of the reasons bears sleep in alders is the protection from the elements they provide. By choosing a dense alder patch sloping in the right direction, you can often find a spot that provides protection from a strong wind and even a driving rain. This is also a good thing to remember in case you get stuck out overnight without a tent.

Choosing a spotting knob with a favorable wind direction is not always practical. Some locations—like ocean beaches or major drainages—will have predominant wind directions that should be used to your advantage. The wind patterns in most areas are unpredictable from day to day so in these situations you will just ignore this criterion when selecting a spotting knob.

Once you have chosen a knob and picked the spot with the best view on the knob, you can customize it. Occasionally, there will be natural windbreaks that also allow you an unobstructed view. However, most of the time, the spot with the best view is a hilltop or hillside that is exposed to the wind and rain. Since it is best to look in an upwind direction, where bears are least likely to get your scent, you will spend a lot of time looking directly into any wind or wind-driven rain. There are a few good ways to protect yourself from these elements.

If land regulations allow in your hunting area, you can dig in and really improve your comfort and chances of success. I often make a bear blind, which looks pretty much like a duck blind, to sit in while glassing for bears. By cutting out blocks of tundra (a short-handled spade works well for this) and then stacking them around the blind, you won't have to dig down very far to create a wind-proof blind. You can also use brush or a tarp to block wind and rain, but you will have to tie the tarp down well or Alaska's winds will shred it in a hurry. The more comfortable you can make yourself on your spotting knob, the more alert you can stay and the better you will be at spotting bears–and that can make all the difference in your success.

I've guided hunters who, despite being instructed about which warm gear to bring, were cold during half of the hunt. As a result, they were not very good bear spotters. I've also had a few hunters who were very good spotters because they stayed warm enough to keep looking. The more comfortable I can make hunters on the spotting knob, the better job they do of helping me find bears.

Dressing in layers to remain comfortably warm and to control your temperature when you are moving is always an advantage for hunters. It is particularly important for spot and stalk bear hunters because this hunting method for brown bears can more aptly be dubbed spot and run, which is more descriptive of what you will actually do. Plan ahead so you can stay as warm and dry as possible at the spotting location, but be dressed so you can remove layers of clothing quickly when you need to travel fast to reach a moving bear. This will often mean stripping down to a light, wind- and water-proof layer with only one light layer underneath.

*Staying as dry and warm as possible is one of the never-ending challenges of bear hunting in Alaska. This hunter is managing, but just barely.*

If the weather is dry, even if it is cool, you may only wear the light under-layer on a stalk. Remember to keep your hat and gloves handy, as these are the best temperature regulators you have. Putting them on will really warm you up, and taking them off at the right time will keep you from unnecessary perspiration that can later chill you off too much.

If your under-layer of clothing does get soaked with perspiration on the stalk, think ahead so you can stay warm. During any rest stops where you will be exposed to wind or chilling temperatures, immediately put on more dry layers so you don't get too chilled. A little cooling is actually ideal to slow or stop your perspiration, but don't let yourself get overly chilled, to the point of shivering, because this is the first sign of hypothermia, which is hard to recover from even when you resume walking.

When you are perspiring profusely and expect to stop for some time—to skin a bear, glass for bears, or sit in camp—you should also think ahead. You can strip down to your last layer just before you stop so that it dries while you walk. Plan this so you are cooling off while drying your clothes, because once you stop, you can immediately put on enough layers to warm back up. If it is too cool to wear just the wet layer(s), you can remove them while you are still warm and moving, put on dry layers next to your skin, then the wet layer(s) on the outside. Wet, synthetic clothes worn on the outside like this will dry quickly even in cool temperatures. By doing this you can have all your layers dry when you reach your stopping point. If any of your wet layers are cotton or wool, these drying techniques will work somewhat, but they will take longer and still retain some, or all, of the moisture. I strongly recommend synthetics for at least your under-layers of clothing, and synthetics for every layer is best.

Because the larger, wiser boars are more nocturnal, the best times for you to spot large bears are early mornings or late evenings. The first hour of daylight and the last three to four hours of daylight are the most productive times to spot a bear. I often spot large bears in the first or last minutes of the day. As a hunter, the ideal time to spot a bear is the first hour of the day, because then you will have all day to complete a successful stalk. If you do spot a bear late at night when there is insufficient time to reach the bear, pay close attention to where he came from and where he is headed, right up until you can't see him any more. That bear may well return to the same daytime hideout the next morning and give you a clue as to where to be watching for him.

On one of my fall-season, Peninsula hunts, we spotted a large boar right at dusk. It was sitting on its haunches, resting just like a dog. I guessed that it just woke up, came out of a nearby alder patch, and was getting ready for a night of foraging. We didn't have enough light to catch the boar that night, so we were on our spotting knob before first light the next morning, looking for that bear.

*When I woke this bear up from a nap, he was fighting mad, but he eventually tried to slip out downwind–right to this waiting hunter.*

He had come out of an alder patch three miles from the beach and was pointed toward the ocean when last we saw him the night before, so we paid close attention to the three mile stretch between the beach and the alders he most likely came from. At first light, we spotted him two miles away, coming off the beach. He was headed for the first alder patches about one-half mile from the beach. Two minutes after we spotted the bear, he disappeared among some alders. If we hadn't been looking right there in those two minutes, we never would have seen this bear.

A couple hours later, we had zigzagged across the two miles of streams and swamps to reach his "bear condo" (as the longtime Alaskan Master Guide Dick Gunlogson calls these alder patches). We ended up forcing the bear out of his bed and harvesting a nice, ten-footer for our efforts.

On another fall-season, Peninsula hunt, during our first six days of hunting, we watched from one location that was just fifteen minutes from our tent. We knew there was a large bear in the area because of the abundant sign we saw. The seventh morning, five minutes into our morning walk to our spotting knob, we spotted a ten-foot boar ghosting through the predawn fog. He was headed for a bed in the alders, but had stayed out just a little too long for his own good. We quickly cut him off, and my client had an easy 100-yard, broadside shot at an unsuspecting bear in the early dawn light.

*This ten-foot Alaska Peninsula bear was trying to slip back to his alder retreat when we spotted him in the early morning fog. He has an unusually high hump for Peninsula brown bears.*

In hunting areas with heavy hunting pressure, it is particularly crucial that fall-season bear hunters be glassing in the first and last few minutes of daylight, for these are the only moments of daylight when many of the large boars are active. When I do spot them in the first light of morning, I can almost feel their anxiety about being out so "late" in the morning. I'm sure the older boars know hunters are daytime animals so they are in danger anytime they can be seen.

One early morning just as the light was coming up, I watched one old boar burst out of a streambed with a fish still in his mouth. He was so concerned about the approaching light he dropped his fish and raced for the safety of the alders–with no one chasing him, just his fear urging him to flee. We watched him run full-speed for the full half-mile to the nearest alder patch.

The older, wiser brown bears on the Alaska Peninsula, Kodiak Island, and some Southeast beaches all display a tendency to be nocturnal during the fall hunting season. In areas of Alaska where there is light hunting pressure, this nocturnal habit is not nearly so pronounced. There are many remote areas in Alaska that see few bear hunters, or maybe none at all for a span of years. Since bears aren't naturally nocturnal, although they can be active night or day, without hunters to make daylight activity more dangerous, they have no reason to become strictly nocturnal. I've seen brown bears in remote areas of the Brooks Range and the Wrangell Mountains that seem to have no fear of people because they haven't learned to be afraid. Bear hunters who pursue bears like these anywhere in Alaska don't need to be nearly as concerned with hunting the earliest and latest hours, although bears still tend to be more active at these times.

Another good time to spot bears is immediately after a bad storm, in either spring or fall. Even bears will feed less when winds hit fifty miles per hour and wind-driven rain or snow make activity less comfortable or productive. Hunters should be out immediately after such weather breaks to watch for hungry bears. At these times, bears will also tend to spend more time feeding in daylight hours to catch up on calorie consumption.

As is the case when hunting any species, becoming a good bear spotter takes some practice. First, you must have a good concept of what a bear, or any part of a bear, looks like from any angle and in any light. When glassing, keep these images in your mind as you scour the tundra, alder patches, beaches, mountainsides, etc. for bear-like objects and parts. Good spotters look for those bear-like parts, not just entire bears. Anyone can spot a clearly visible bear, but it takes a little imagination and practice to identify a bear from just a small, visible piece of the bear.

I spotted one bear at a couple miles by noticing a small bump of tundra that had an unusual color to it. After watching it for thirty minutes, the bump turned out to be a bear's head, the only part that was visible. The sun shining through the fur had looked golden brown, which was the only clue it wasn't just another bump on the tundra.

I've also spotted several "quill bears." The shape and walking motion of a porcupine are identical to that of a bear. At a distance, when you don't have nearby objects to gauge size, porcupines look like bears on the tundra. It is always exciting for a few seconds to imagine you've spotted a trophy bear, before you realize (or your hunting buddy unsympathetically points out) it's another one of those "quill bears."

Bears are very short animals (for their bulk) that typically walk with their heads down. Large bears can walk across tabletop-flat terrain and be completely hidden, or almost so, in the slight irregularities in the surface. Sometimes only their humps show up above the tundra as they move along. It takes concentration to pick out these parts of

*This spring-season nine-footer was unusually gaunt for a large bear. Perhaps he wasn't skilled at finding food, there were many other, larger bears in the area, or the salmon run was weak the previous fall.*

bears that look just like the other thousands of bumps in the tundra, but this is sometimes all that is visible–at first.

Many times, we only glimpse a bear for a minute or two, at a distance of a mile or more, and then it comes into full view. It may then disappear from view entirely, and not be visible again. We may only have a few minutes to spot these bears, and we have to be looking in the exact spot at the precise time to do so. By identifying the humps, backs, or backsides of possible bears and keeping close tabs on these until they move, you will spot a lot more bears, especially when your spotting knob has a view for several miles in all directions. Many times, we have scored on bears like this that were clearly visible for less than five minutes. One of the crucial skills of a good bear hunter is being an exceptional bear spotter. A hunter's spotting skills frequently determine the outcome of a hunt.

## SPRING HUNTING

Wherever you hunt brown bears in Alaska, the bears are different in the spring season. They are not nearly as alert, and completely nocturnal bears are rare. Even on the hottest days—up to 70 degrees during some springs—I have seen large boars active in the heat of the day. They seem to be so hungry and/or groggy from a long winter's sleep, they ignore their normal instincts for self-preservation. Of course, this doesn't mean these large bears are easy to hunt, just not quite as difficult as in fall when they are fully alert.

Spring is also mating season for bears. The first problem that arises for hunters is how to identify a mating couple, versus a sow with a large cub. One of the first clues is when the smaller of the two bears is leading. Cubs seldom lead their sows, but sows are often in the lead of a mating pair. Another good clue is the interaction between the pair. Sows will play a little with older cubs, but mating pairs display a lot more interaction:  they play, they stand front to front, they stand front to back, they chase each other, and they mate.

I once watched a pair of large bears that I was hoping were a mating couple. The smaller bear had to be at least 300 pounds and the larger one was twice that size. After an hour passed and I was about to take my hunter after these bears, the sow sat on her butt and the large cub nursed. This could have been a two-year-old cub, which would make either bear legal, but we had no desire to shoot a nursing sow.

*Spotting mating pairs in spring season is not unusual. However, this is a sow (on the bank) and her two and one-half year old cub. Even if you were not sure in this case, it is obvious neither bear is large (see Chapter Nine, "Judging Bears").*

Another way to identify mating pairs is by looking closely at each bear for sex and size clues. Typically (but not always), the larger bear is the boar so I look for large, male characteristics: the male head shape, the length of the neck, the head to body ratio, etc. (see Chapter Two, "Bear Biology," or Chapter Nine, "Judging Bears"). If I decide the large bear is at least nine feet, it almost has to be a male, so I am looking at a mating pair, not a sow and cub.

Next, I look at the smaller bear. Sometimes, I can iden- tify it as an eight-foot-plus, female-looking bear. The largest cubs I've seen are no more than seven feet, so a bear that looks like an eight-footer is most likely an adult. Sometimes, I can see the smaller bear has several cub-like features (see Chapter Two, "Bear Biology"), even from a couple miles' distance.

Whatever I decide about a pair of bears in spring, I won't finalize my decision until I get a close look at them from shooting distance. It is seldom easy to identify mating pairs, and I certainly won't shoot unless I'm positive. We once watched what we thought were two older cubs (neither were over seven-feet) for almost an hour before they suddenly displayed mating activity. This was on the Peninsula where bears grow large at a young age. However, neither were over three hundred pounds and both still had cub-like features, but they were definitely mating.

In places where brown or grizzly bears seldom exceed eight feet, it is much harder to identify mating pairs. It is more difficult to pick out sex characteristics on six- and seven-foot bears, than it is on nine- and ten-foot bears. In those areas with smaller bears, hunters will just have to pass on pairs of bears in spring if these can't be positively identified.

During spring mating season, lone sows in heat will urinate on their back legs and feet. Wherever they walk, they will leave a scent trail for boars to find. Any boar crossing these trails will usually get outwardly excited and hurriedly follow the sow's trail. Attentive hunters will notice this immediate change in a bear's behavior. If the boar is worth going after, a hunter that noted which way the sow went, will know where the boar is headed and realize it will get there in a hurry.

Sows with cubs will also leave their scent trail, but this scent will mean something else to boars–food. Large boars learn that first- or second-year cubs are easy prey.

*Large boars like this Kodiak monster are always on the lookout for cubs to eat, but this is most prevalent in early spring when food is scarce (28 0/16 B&C).*

Boars crossing the scent trail of sows with cubs in spring will get just as excited and move just as fast as if they had crossed the trail of a sow-in-heat.

During one spring hunt, we had a boar come right to us on a sow and cub's trail. We had watched the bear come our direction for several miles down a snowfield, displaying the common springtime stupor of a bear just out of the den. He would stop at times and just lie down to rest on the snow for five to ten minutes. When he hit the trail of the two bears, he was immediately energized: his head came up, his body came alive, and he fast-walked and galloped right to where we were waiting on the sow's trail.

Boars that are following a sow in heat or a sow with a cub will usually be so excited they are not as alert as they should be. Their focus is obviously on one thing, catching that sow or the cub with its sow. But, the boar will be moving very fast so hunters will have less time to cut it off, and will have to be ready to shoot quickly because the bear will seldom break his stride until he gets very close to his objective or loses the scent trail.

Older boars also look for sows with cubs that are still near, or in, their dens. The cubs are one of the earliest sources of high-quality food in the spring before hillsides have greened or even been exposed. Boars will either separate the cubs from their sow or even dig out sows with cubs still in their winter dens. Occasionally the boars will even kill the sows to get at the cubs.

We once watched a large boar attempting to get at three newborn cubs. The sow had the cubs near the sharp peak of a six-thousand foot mountain trying to stay away from the boar. The upper half of the mountain was covered in snow and ice. The boar kept sliding down the steep, icy slope— as much as 1,000 feet at a time—in his attempts to get to the cubs. Finally, the sow maneuvered her tiny cubs to the very top of the peak and over the top and the boar gave up, at least for that day, then he slid and crawled down the steep, icy slope to the exposed hillside below. We watched all this from over four miles, but even those tiny cubs were clearly visible in our spotting scope against the snowy mountain.

Even though boars will sometimes kill sows to get at the cubs, brown bears will seldom eat other adult brown bears, although they will eat black bears of any size. Of all the bear carcasses I have watched, I have never seen a brown bear carcass that was fed on by another brown bear. Master Guide Dick Gunlogson has never seen a brown bear feed on another adult brown bear carcass in his 30+ years of guiding on the Alaska Peninsula. I've heard it does happen, but it must be a rare occurrence. Even though brown bears will seldom feed on brown bear carcasses, they are not spooked by an earlier brown bear kill in their area, unless they smell any leftover human odor.

*Spring bears can be found on the beaches, in the river bottoms where there is no snow, or on the snowy tops of mountains, but they are much more visible against a snowy background.*

Spring bear spotting should include close scrutiny of snowfields. Not only can good spotters spot bears over five miles away, they can also read the trails left by the bears. The staggered, roundish post-hole tracks left by traveling bears are easily identifiable after just minimal practice. Sometimes, visually following these trails will lead a hunter's eyes right to a bear–back on his den or resting on the snow. These trails will often cross miles of snow before the bear is spotted. At several miles, brown bears look like tiny, roundish dots on the snow, and their movements may be barely perceptible even after minutes of close scrutiny. But many times, spotting such a bear at several miles has led me to a successful stalk later that day or the next. Bears will travel miles and miles in one day and sometimes bee-line straight at waiting hunters.

Snowfields are very productive glassing areas because bears can be spotted easily at great distances and their trails can tell hunters about activity and the direction of travel. By monitoring tracks day-to-day, hunters can concentrate their glassing efforts along new tracks to find the bears that made them. If few or no new tracks are appearing, hunters may need to move their spotting knob, or their camp, to find the bears.

Locating and hunting bears near their dens in spring is possible for diligent hunters. In fall, bears choose denning spots that will soon be covered with snow and will remain covered long enough in spring until there is sufficient food available to sustain them. An ideal denning spot to meet these requirements would be a northern-facing slope, that is also a leeward slope that drifts over in early winter, with an overhang that enhances drifting and protects the den from the spring sun. Seldom does one den meet all these ideals, but most brown bear dens meet at least one of these three objectives.

Most brown bear dens are spotted in spring by the dirty bear tracks on the snow, radiating out from the mouth of the den. Bears seldom desert their den immediately upon coming out the first time. They will usually dig out, then at least hang around the entrance to wake up a little. Older boars tend to leave quicker, and earlier in the spring, than sows with cubs (or lone sows out of habit), but there are usually visible, dirty tracks near dens before the bear leaves for good. The bear, or bears, can often be seen lying in the mouth of the den, resting before they leave for good.

The problems with trying to bag a brown bear at or near the den are determining size, hide quality, and sex. Bears that are spotted lying in the mouth or near the den are difficult to judge accurately. Even if hunters take a chance and travel up to the den, hoping it is a good bear, and all of the bear is visible outside the den, the bear will be difficult to judge if it doesn't stand up. Without getting a few min-

*The cover photo of this book shows how obvious bear tracks on the snow can be. They sink in deeply and are staggered side to side more than any other animal, so they can be identified from many miles.*

utes to look over the hide, even if it does stand up, you cannot be sure the off side is not badly rubbed.

The most crucial unknown about a bear near a den is whether it has cubs. If it is obviously a ten-foot boar, you are safe. But anything less might possibly be a sow with cubs. Sows will wander as much as a few hundred yards from the den without their cubs. Even if you have seen a bear near a den for days and no cubs appear, they may still be inside. I would want to see, or have seen, the bear walk at least 400 yards away from the den without cubs to be sure it was legal and to also get a good enough look to determine its size and hide quality.

## FOOD SOURCES

Although brown bears will eat just about anything edible, their natural foods are grasses, sedges, horsetails, cow parsnips, various roots, berries of all kinds, ground squirrels, fish, and carrion. Some bears learn to be efficient predators on newborn caribou and moose calves, and some of the larger, more experienced bears are even capable of taking adult moose.

Some of the first foods exploited by many bears in spring are roots of various plants and the first grasses and sedges. Slide runways produced by avalanches or rock slides create exposed hillsides where these foods will be available in early spring. South-facing slopes, or any slopes facing the predominant, spring winds are the first to be exposed in spring. These are good spots for spring bear hunters to concentrate their attention.

Ocean, river and lake beaches all provide grazing grounds for brown bears from spring through fall. The grasses, sedges, and horsetails on these beaches are mainly utilized in spring when the vegetation is young and the most nutritious. Bears foraging on beach vegetation will usually feed for thirty minutes to two hours and move around slowly during that time. Sunken water channels, or fringing bushes

*Salmon are a favorite food of bears, but they are omnivores, which means they will eat almost anything that is edible.*

or forests can provide the cover hunters need to stalk these bears. Even the largest bears can be shy about feeding too far away from cover, so they will typically stay fairly close to the fringes when using large, open beach grasslands.

Brown bears can also be shy about feeding too far away from cover in large berry patches, particularly in areas with high hunting pressure. Berry bushes will often cover the same slide-cleared slopes that produce the first roots and grasses in early spring for bears. When feeding on berries, brown bears usually feed on the move. If berries are dense enough, bears may slow down almost to a standstill, but where berries are sparsely scattered, bears can be moving almost as fast as hunters can walk.

Hunters should first observe feeding bears closely to determine how fast they are moving, then decide what angle would be needed to cut off the bear, and then decide if a stalk is even feasible. An interception point of a mile or two in front of a fast-moving bear feeding on berries is not un-common. The longer the lead you need to give a moving bear, the more chance it will change course and the stalk will fail. Anytime you make a failed stalk, you risk spook-ing that bear, any previously unseen bears you spook dur-ing the stalk, or future bears that cross your scent trail. You also stop looking for more bears if you engage in a long-shot stalk on a fast-moving, distant bear.

Brown bears in spring and fall also cruise beaches in search of food. They dig for crustaceans, insects, clams and eat a variety of organic matter that washes up on beaches. Any large sea mammals—like sea lions, walrus, and whales—that wash up on the beach are a great find for a bear, or bears. Dead whales are a great find for bear hunters because there will usually be a number of bears feeding on the carcass for days, or even weeks. Individual bears that feed on a whale for several days or more will usually have a pattern of where they bed and how they travel to get there. This allows observant hunters the chance to wait in ambush for a particular bear. Often an ambush is the best choice on large carcasses because the wind is wrong, there is no cover, or there are just too many bears to stalk close enough for a shot at the best trophy.

When you are hunting salmon streams for fishing bears, the optimal situation to look for is a favorite fishing spot. Favorite bear fishing spots are typically taken over by the larger bears who chase away the smaller bears. Plus, all but the meanest sows will choose to keep their cubs away from large bears that pose a real threat to the cubs. One of the most difficult tasks is finding such a spot without contami-nating it with human scent. Ideally, you should do your search at least a week before your hunt or even during the previous season so your scent doesn't spook bears to other fishing sites.

*Because bears are often intent on fishing and not alert to danger, it is possible for hunters to get very close to them. This large boar is selecting a meal from the dozens of salmon splashing in front of him.*

If you do walk a waterway to find the good fishing sites, sometimes this can be accomplished from an upper stream bank with the aid of binoculars. Even from 100 yards you can see the fish jaws, gill plates, and bones left by feeding bears. Significant accumulations of these fish parts are pretty easy to spot if the bear has been feeding in the open. If the banks are brushy or the bears feel the hunting pressure, they may carry their fish into the brush to feed, and there may be little visible evidence you can see from any distance, so you may have to engage in a close-up search.

If you have to walk near or in the stream to search for evidence of feeding bears, it is better to stay in the water, and definitely don't touch anything. The less scent you leave behind, the better your chances of not spooking any bears.

If you are hunting where there are only a few salmon for the bears, because it is early or late in the season or the salmon run is weak, there may not be any specific, productive fishing spots for the bears. In these cases, you may just find a lookout where you can watch for cruising bears, or cruise the stream yourself if no such lookout exists. If there are gulls in the area, they will often make a ruckus when a bear is fishing below them. By looking for these squawking, flying gulls you can often save time and cut straight to the spot where a bear is fishing.

It is less tiring (physically), faster, and quieter to go downstream while cruising a stream, but you must watch the wind. Unless there is a stiff upstream or cross-stream breeze that actually gets right down on the water, the water flow will create a downstream air flow and slowly carry your scent ahead of you. Anytime the streambed is surrounded by high brush or a tall bank, the on-stream air flow may be different than that of the air even ten feet over the water. Pay close attention to air flow whenever you walk along sheltered streambeds, or along any trough-like route, if you don't want to send your scent ahead of you to spook bears.

When brown bears make a kill or find a carcass that is too large for them to eat at one sitting, they usually cover it with any convenient vegetation. This marks it as theirs, physically protects it from small scavengers, and accelerates the rotting process to make it more appealing and digestible for them. They may even lie on top of a fresh kill to protect it, which may cause their body heat to hasten the rotting process.

These carcass mounds may be only a few feet high and a few feet wide, or they may be ten feet high and twenty feet wide. They are usually identifiable because of the exposed earth and obvious excavation for many feet around the mound. Hunters can sometimes spot these mounds on the open tundra from some distance by the unnatural dark peat on and around the mound. Eagles, magpies, ravens, and crows nearby can also indicate the presence of a carcass mound. If the birds are staying a short distance away or acting nervous, this can mean the bear is very near. Fox and coyotes are also common scavengers on kills and likewise can help hunters locate carcass mounds. The nervous stares of fox can sometimes help observant hunters find a bedded bear.

*This bear was found feeding on a whale carcass—a great find for bear hunters. There were several bears feeding on the whale, so the hunters simply selected the largest one (it's never quite that simple).*

Brown bears that make kills and don't finish eating a carcass in late fall may mound the remaining food to keep it for next spring. If the mound is large enough and freezes quickly, it may be impenetrable to wolves, wolverines and other winter scavengers. The maker of the mound will then have spring food as soon as he wakes from hibernation.

If a carcass mound is out in the open, a bear may find a bed from a few feet to several hundred yards away in heavy brush to sleep between meals. No matter how far away the bear beds, it will be alert for anything or anybody that tries

*This is why bear hunters always have to be sure of their target. It would be a shame to orphan these cubs. When you hunt carcass mounds or dens you must be extra careful to watch for cubs before shooting.*

to steal its food. Hunters must be alert when approaching a carcass mound to avoid arousing the bear before they have identified the bear. If it is an undesirable trophy, or a sow with cubs, you do not want to have to deal with an angry bear you don't want to kill. If possible, you should try to spot any bear near a carcass mound from a distance and decide if it is a desirable trophy before you get close enough to risk a charge.

Although glassing from one location is the standard practice among experienced brown bear hunters, like any hunting rule, there are exceptions. An exceptional hunter knows there are situations which require different tactics, even if these tactics defy the accepted practice. If you are hunting an area with a very low bear density, or you are in a very remote area where bears haven't learned to fear hunters yet, or staying put is just not working, you may decide to travel through your hunting area to look for bears. You must have good reasons for this, because most of the time this practice will be a mistake for brown bear hunters.

If you do walk about during a brown bear hunt, try to leave as little scent as possible. Do not touch anything with your bare hands. Surgical gloves used for skinning bears can be worn so your hands don't accidentally leave a strong scent. Always relieve yourself at camp before going, and when you have to relieve yourself while traveling, use pee bottles, cat holes, or whatever means you can think of to keep your scent down. Try to stay out of feeding and bedding areas as much as possible, and do not travel on bear trails unless it is unavoidable. Traveling while glassing for bears can be successful in some situations, but you must always be vigilant about where your scent is being left or carried by the wind.

## CRUISING SHORELINES

Cruising ocean, lake, or large river shorelines for brown bears could be considered another style of spot and stalk hunting. Bear hunters use various-sized watercraft to motor along slowly and glass for bears on the beach. Once a desirable bear is spotted and the wind direction is noted, the hunter(s) put in on the beach and stalk the bruin. It is a simple hunting method, but there are some facts, skills, and habits to learn that will improve your chances of success.

First of all, there are some places this works, and others where it doesn't pay. Cruising ocean beaches is commonly used in southeastern Alaska because there are few large, open areas inland. Forests and brush cover much of the land so beaches are one of the few places with enough visibility to make glassing worthwhile.

On Kodiak Island, where there has been a lot of fishing, hunting, and other human activity for decades, brown bears learn at a young age to be wary on the beaches in daylight hours. Beach hunting is generally poor on Kodiak, and, in fact, the farther inland you are willing to travel, the better your chances for the large Kodiak bears. The one exception is when you can find a dead whale on the beach. Large bears will often risk the dangers of being spotted on the beach in daylight to feed on a plentiful supply of high-quality food such as a washed-up whale carcass.

The early morning and late evening are typically the most productive times to spot any bears on beaches. Often, the last half-hour of light will produce more bears than the entire rest of the day. If you shoot a bear in the last few minutes of daylight, you have to be sure of your shot, have a good backup gun ready, and be ready to take care of the bear immediately if it occurs during an incoming tide.

In Alaska, hunters are not allowed to shoot brown bears from boats moving from engine power. Even if the engine has been shut off, the movement from the engine must have stopped before you may shoot. In much of southeastern Alaska (currently GMU's one through five), you cannot even shoot from a boat unless you have a special handicap permit. As I explained in Chapter Five "Choosing Your Hunting Area," brown bear hunters must always thoroughly examine the current hunting regulations before beginning their hunt.

Hunters should try to cruise beaches in an upwind direction whenever possible. If you do have to travel while upwind of a bear, moving outside a cove or simply several hundred yards off the beach will often keep your scent away from the beach. You should also try to cruise in a way that keeps the sun at your back, and not in your eyes. The difference between looking into the sun for bears on the beach or having a well-lit beach with the sun at your back is amazing. You will spot a lot more bears in the latter case.

Bears that are spotted on a beach may be there a few minutes and then disappear into the brush for no apparent

*In Southeast, cruising shorelines is sometimes the only viable way to spot bears. The timber is thick and there are few openings to glass for bears. The beaches are about the only open areas to watch.*

reason, or they may walk the beach for miles. If they do disappear, you can sometimes find them by scouting ahead to see if they reappear farther along the beach. They often have well-worn trails that cut across points of land or around river mouths. They may not reappear for more than a half-mile or more, but it is worth your time to pause long enough to see if a trophy-size bear reappears in these situations. Bears are also creatures of habit. If you see a good bear on a beach, but it disappears before you can finish a stalk, you may get another chance at that bear on another day if you return to the same beach at the same time.

When you are hunting on ocean beaches in Alaska you must remember how large a variation there can be between high and low tide. This variation can be 25 feet or more, and the entire change from the two extremes happens in six hours. The speed at which the water flows to accomplish these great variations between tides is amazing, even to those of us who have seen it firsthand. If you are many miles up a long inlet from the mouth, the water will flow even faster than if you are in a shorter bay.

When hunting Alaska's beaches with watercraft you should always carry a tide book and refer to it every day. You will need to carry long ropes and an anchor for your boat, at the least. Experienced boaters devise anchor, rope, and pulley systems to enable them to keep their boats afloat at all times. Some beaches have such shallow slopes that your choices are: let the boat/skiff go dry and then wait for the next high tide to float it; plan to drop off the hunter(s) to stalk a bear and then leave someone on the boat to motor back out to deep water; or have a skiff that can be used to reach the beach and leave the larger boat anchored far enough offshore to remain afloat.

The same extreme tides and shallow beaches will also trap careless hunters on foot. You must always examine any beaches before you begin a stalk so you can plan your drop-off and pick-up times and places. An incoming tide can quickly cut you off from your skiff or exit point and even trap you on an island of beach. This can result in a little inconvenience, or a life-threatening situation. In fact, drownings are one of the primary causes of accidental deaths in Alaska.

If you are camping on an ocean beach in Alaska, you must also deal with the tides. Exceptionally high tides or normal tides that are wind-driven can swamp hunting camps that are placed too close to the beach. Carefully examine any potential camp location to verify that it does not occasionally get flooded. The highest flotsam or driftwood will tell you what level the highest tides have reached. Camp above that level.

*Choosing a stand location is the most important aspect of this type of hunting. The height, the placement, the wind direction, the sun angle, and many more aspects must be considered. Serious hunters can learn a tremendous amount from consulting a (whitetail) deer hunters' handbook on stand-hunting. The good manuals contain incredible amounts of detail, much of which is useful for bear hunters wishing to hunt from a treestand.*

## STAND-HUNTING

The three most common places to stand-hunt for bears are on a salmon stream, on a carcass mound, or on the remnants of a big game kill. Bowhunters most often stand-hunt, but firearms hunters can also use this hunting method when it is appropriate for the situation. Some of these situations are: when it is too brushy to spot-and-stalk or walk streams effectively, when there is a fresh kill in an area where food sources are sparse, and when a very desirable bear was spooked away from a carcass but will likely come back.

The number one rule for effective stand-hunting is to watch your scent. If you are in one place for a long time, particularly if you are in an elevated stand, it is easy to stink up the area with human scent. Winds can change many times during the day, you will have to relieve yourself, you will have to eat, and it is easy to leave your human scent by touching trees, brush, and grass–all of which lessen the chances of spotting a good bear. Effective stand-hunters must limit the odors they produce, wear gloves whenever they climb trees or rearrange brush, and hunt stands only when the wind directions are favorable.

Choose stand locations that will permit good shot opportunities, but not if they compromise the chances of even seeing bears. Your approach to and departure from the stand must be carefully planned. You should not walk through bear bedding areas or along trails or routes bears will likely use. Your routes should also be quiet enough not to alert bears when you come or go. Some locations look great at first glance because there is abundant sign nearby, but if you cannot reach the stand without spooking every bear in the area, it is not worth hunting. Some stands can only be hunted when the wind direction is from one point of the compass. Others may only be good for morning or evening stands if that is when bears travel by that location. Careful study of an area is vital in order to choose effective stands.

One of the most difficult factors to learn about a possible stand location is when the bears are present. I once set up a stand on a promising salmon stream with plenty of

*Finding sign where bears have been feeding on salmon is the first criterion for placing a stand on a stream. However, hunters must do this without leaving scent that will spook the larger bears, and ruin the area for hunting.*

bear sign. It wasn't until my fifth trip in to my stand that I discovered a heavily used fishermen's trail. No wonder I didn't see many bears there in daylight hours. Any large bears in the area had learned to visit that spot at night, to avoid the bothersome fishermen with their noisy, bear protection guns. I needed to move away from the favorite human fishing holes, to where bears had more privacy and felt safer in daylight hours. I used that lesson when I placed my future stand.

## SNOWMACHINE HUNTING

Spring snowmachine hunting for brown bears is legal in Alaska, but you cannot chase bears on the machines. As soon as a bear is aware of hunters on snowmachines, the hunters have to stop moving toward the bear. Bears will usually hear an approaching snowmachine more than a mile away, unless there is a geographic feature (like a mountain) preventing sound from reaching their ears. Hunters cannot pursue the bear on the machine or try to drive it or herd it toward waiting hunters. They also cannot shoot while on the machine, even if it has been shut off.

Snowmachines can be used effectively to travel to a location where you can then hunt on foot or even to search daily for bears, and then continue on foot once the bear has been spotted. Snowmachine hunting requires an early spring hunt to ensure enough snow remains after the hunt to get back out. The starting point for the machines is often at a much lower elevation than the hunt area. The snow at the starting point will usually be gone or too rotten to travel over well before the snow in the hunt area deteriorates to that point. If there is not enough snow to get the machines out after the hunt, you may have to leave them and plan to come back weeks later when the ground is firm enough for off-road land vehicles—if they are permitted in that area and can physically reach the machines and then carry them out.

Snowmachine hunters always need to carry quality snowshoes for stalking bears or for walking out if the machine breaks down. Snowmachine hunters should also travel in pairs at all times for safety reasons. Overflow, weak ice, and avalanches are some of the more prevalent dangers that plague all spring hunters.

Hunters who can overcome the many drawbacks of bear hunting on snowmachines can often hunt some otherwise inaccessible areas. Early bears are also likely to be large boars with good hides. Snowmachine hunters are also more mobile than drop-off hunters or even hunters with airplanes, as a good rider astride an off-trail machine can cover a lot of ground while winter snows still cover much of the brush and terrain irregularities.

Bear hunting has a unique allure to it because of the inherent dangers involved. Bear hunters are drawn to hunt these great animals for a number of reasons. A few hunters actually understand bear hunting. It is not an ego trip; it is a personal journey to meet the challenge–physically and mentally. Some hunters arrive at this point, many never will. Bear hunting should not be viewed as a personal quest for status, an ego trip, or a keep-up-with-the-Joneses attitude. It takes the right hunter who can appreciate the process of gaining a respect and admiration of these great animals. As with most types of hunting, it is the process that is important, not the killing.

*This spring-season Kodiak bear was found in the river bottom, which makes packing much easier than when they are on the tops of the mountains (26 1/16 B&C).*

*"The trail is the thing, not the end of the trail. Travel too fast and you miss all you are traveling for."* –Louis L'Amour

*The big bears are impressive, right down to their toes.*

# 8
# STALKING BEARS

*"Life is not holding a good hand; life is playing a poor hand well."* –Danish Proverb

Once you've spotted a bear that appears to be a desirable trophy, you must decide whether to attempt a stalk. This is one of the most important decisions of the hunt. It is also one of the most difficult. Every bit of hunting experience and knowledge you and your hunting companions have should be used to make this decision. There is no formula for making this decision. It is one of those times when you need to really become a hunter, in every sense of the word, and make the best decision.

## INITIAL ANALYSIS

The variables to consider when deciding whether or not to stalk a brown bear are:
- which way the bear is traveling;
- how fast it is going;
- how fast you can travel;
- what geographic obstacles are in the way;
- how much daylight is left;
- which way the wind is blowing;
- how predictable the winds are;
- how many hunting days you have left;
- how desirable the bear is;
- how much you trust your initial judgment of the bear;
- and how many bears you have been seeing each day.

Evaluating all of these elements, plus any others unique to the situation, asking the right questions and coming up with the right answers, and doing all this without being unduly influenced by emotions is one of the most difficult aspects of bear hunting. Your decision can easily make or break a hunt and determine what trophy you go home with, or if you take anything home at all. You can't just decide to chase every bear you see, and likewise, you can't hold off on any bear that doesn't walk right up to you. A good bear hunter will make a careful, analytical decision, and make it quickly.

Smart hunters will begin a careful analysis of their hunting area from the first minute they arrive. By noting slopes, rivers, cliffs, ravines, snowfields, avalanche chutes, brush patches, areas providing easy travel routes, etc., you can be prepared to make quicker stalking decisions. You can also make note of any prevailing wind patterns, when the morning and evening thermals begin, and areas where swirling winds are likely. Make mental notes of how fast you are moving each time you travel anywhere to get a feel for your ground speed.

It is also very helpful to begin to make a mental map of your hunting area from day one. By noting landmarks and distances between them, you are more prepared to make a quick mental calculation of how fast you can cover ground on a stalk. Having a map of landmarks in your head will also help you keep track of your movements compared to those of a bear once you are on a stalk. It is very easy to get temporarily confused about your location during a stalk and lose precious minutes while you regain your bearings. Any minutes you lose can easily cost you a chance at a good bear, and may be the reason you go home empty-handed. Begin assimilating your hunting ground's characteristics immediately. It is one of the marks of any good hunter.

*Brown bears can live to be 20 or 30 years old. In that many years, they learn a lot and become fairly elusive. Most of the time, any hunter who bags a bear like this one has earned it by outsmarting the bear (26 1/16 B&C).*

## MAKE A PLAN

Once you have decided to stalk a bear, make a plan and make contingent plans to allow for changes in the bear's direction or speed and to allow for unforeseen obstacles or wind changes. This is where you should use all the information you have gathered about the area.

Of course the dominant factor when you plan your stalk is: don't let the bear scent you. Follow this rule and 90 percent of your stalks on brown bears can be successful. Brown bears can smell odors over a mile away (ADF&G, 1). After hunters spend a week in a bear camp without a shower, I don't doubt bears can smell them over two miles away. Not letting the bear scent you is pretty basic bear hunting knowledge, but how you apply this is what determines your success as a bear hunter.

You should imagine that air is flowing like a river, which it does, but you just can't see it. There are main flows, side channels, and back eddies. The main currents are the predominant winds caused by weather systems. The side channels are either thermals that move in different directions than the main flow, or parts of the main flows that are diverted or funneled by ridgelines, ravines, bluffs, or any large terrain features. The back eddies appear at the intersections of two or more air flows or near the edges of any large terrain features.

What all these possibilities for air movements mean for hunters is:  you should monitor air movements continually during a stalk. You can carry a powder bottle (or use dry grass) to determine air movements that are too light to feel. You can look around you and ahead of you (with your binoculars when necessary) to determine air movements by noting how vegetation is moving, how low-flying birds are affected, how airborne debris is moving, or how ripples are moving on water surfaces.

In strong winds, your downwind scent will spread out over a narrow, but widening funnel-shaped area. In light winds, your downwind scent will spread out over a wider, and ever-widening funnel-shaped area. Any terrain features are going to disturb this downwind, funnel-shaped scent trail you leave. Larger features will disturb it more than smaller features. Some features, combined with strong thermals can even carry your scent upward away from the ground's surface, where they will harmlessly dissipate. That is why bears who are directly downwind of you will occasionally not scent you.

It is impossible to predict all the vagaries of air movements, but it is still practical to make the best guess each time you plan and execute a stalk. My best recommendation is to be conservative whenever possible. When you have

*This Brooks Range grizzly ignored our scent on a moose kill and actually came toward us on our spotting knob to challenge us for the remains. This is one of the few situations when your scent may not play a factor on a bear hunt.*

the time and you think a bear may smell you if you go one way, make a detour that will reduce the odds of being scented. It takes discipline to decide to take a longer, tougher route on a stalk, but this is often the only way you will be successful.

When you have a bear spotted, the first observation to make is what direction any strong wind is blowing. Then, imagine which way the warm (uphill) or cool (downhill) thermals are going. Taking into account the strength of the predominant wind and the thermals, you can then imagine how odors are being moved over the entire distance between you and the bear. Plan a route that prevents the bear from scenting you, plus alternative routes to use if the situation changes.

The speed a bear is moving is a very important factor in your decision whether to stalk the bear or pass on it. Bears that are moving back and forth to known food sources— like salmon streams, berry patches, or beached whales— tend to move faster than bears that are just foraging for whatever they can find. If a bear's head is in a relaxed, downward position, it will move slower than when its head is up and alert. An exception is when a bear's head is down because it is on the hot trail of a sow, a sow with cubs, or a wounded animal it is trying to catch.

Bears differ in size so much that the larger ones have much longer stride lengths and move much faster, though their feet may move at the same rhythm. Always watch a bear for several minutes to determine its speed before deciding whether to stalk it. This not only helps you decide whether or not to stalk the bear, this will also help you decide where you can intercept the bruin. Always remember that bears can walk or even feed along (on berries or vegetation) at a faster speed than most hunters can sustain for more than an hour or so in typical Alaskan bear country.

It is very difficult to catch a moving bear that is going straight away from you. You can usually catch bears that are walking away at an angle if you have enough time and energy and they aren't too far ahead. I seldom go after a walking bear that is angling away from me if the stalk will cover more than two miles. If I can't catch it in that distance, the odds of losing it are pretty high, so it would only be worth that risk in a few situations, i.e., a huge bear or the last day of the hunt. If a bear is angling toward me, even if it is five miles away, I may go after it immediately if I think it will continue in my direction.

*Even in the short, sparse cover shown here, it is not too difficult for experienced hunters to avoid being spotted by a bear's so-so eyesight. His nose is the thing to watch out for.*

## BEARS' EYESIGHT

A bear's eyesight may become a factor in a stalk when you are within 800 yards. Bears that look in your direction can see you at 800 yards or more if you are moving in the open on a contrasting background. I have walked straight at bears within 200 yards that did not see me–when either my clothing matched the background color or I stayed on the fringes of cover. If you are in yellow grass, typical of many Alaskan countrysides, put on yellow camo or even drape your muslin game bag over you so you blend in. I have turned my raincoat inside out to expose the white lining and crawled across the open snow to within 100 yards of a bear without being spotted. Staying in cover, even short cover that only comes halfway up your height is better than stalking in the open, and stalking along fringes is always a good idea to prevent your silhouette from standing out on a more uniform background.

As with any animals, moving directly at a bear will lessen the chances it will see you. A bear will be much more likely to detect sideways movement. Much of the time, if they are not alarmed, bears will carry their heads down low so they can continually scent the ground for food odors. But if they raise their heads and look, they can see better than you may think. Always freeze if you are within a half-mile when a bear picks its head up and looks in your direction. Keep in mind their eyes are about as good as ours, so you can't totally ignore their eyesight when stalking.

## FOOLING THEIR EARS

Within 800 yards, you must also pay attention to the type and amount of noise you make. Bears will hear footfalls on crunchy snow or twigs snap at several hundred yards, or farther on a windless day. You should have tried out all your equipment beforehand (like any good hunter) to make sure nothing squeaks or rattles. Since shooting ranges tend to be close for bears, noise can play an important part in the success of the final portion of a stalk.

Check out your clothing for anything that will make noise when dragging on brush or on itself. Heavy nylon coats or packs are some of the worst offenders. Experiment with all your gear so you know how to avoid making these sounds. You may have to remove a hopelessly noisy piece of gear as you close in on a bear. You can also carry lightweight, but quiet, covers for your pack, jacket, or pants if necessary.

Hip boots can make loud, bear-alarming sounds when slapped by brush. You can roll them down to expose the

*Fooling a bear's ears is also not too difficult for experienced hunters. Wind and water often make enough noise to cover a hunter's approach in to bow range, even if he or she does make a few mistakes. Bears that are fishing are sometimes very tolerant of noise and even a little tolerant of scent, depending on how involved they are in their quest for food.*

much quieter inside lining or roll them down and cover them with your soft, quiet pants.

You should be able to work the bolt and the safety of the rifle almost noiselessly. Practice before the hunt if you haven't already mastered this skill. The snap of a safety at close range will alert an otherwise unsuspecting bear. By putting your thumb and forefinger on either side of the safety as you ease it forward, you should be able to move it without making a sound.

You should also know how to muffle a cough or sneeze that would otherwise ruin a stalk. Rub your throat to stop a cough; pinch and rub the sides of your nose to stop a sneeze. If you just can't stop either a cough or a sneeze–quickly kneel down, cup your hands on either side of your face, lean forward until your hands touch the ground, and let the earth absorb your cough or sneeze.

## BEACH STALKS

When you are stalking a bear on a beach, there are some unique considerations. First, the wind direction at the head of even a wide cove will often be different than at the mouth. So your planned stalk may end up being directly downwind. In these cases, you can either try to circle inland from the bear and come out downwind of it or stay out on a point where your scent is carried away from the bear and wait for it to move to you.

There are also times when the air movements at the water line versus the grass or timberline at the top of the beach are different. Always pay attention to air movements as you move toward a bear on the beach because they can change at any point in the stalk. You may have to descend to the water line to continue your stalk, but make sure to walk in a crouch and keep your head low; our tall, vertical silhouette is easily discernible and is a dead giveaway to every game animal I know. By walking right on the water line, you will have some background cover to break up your outline. If you are careful to freeze if the bear looks up, you may be able to finish the stalk without the bear sighting you. Often they are so involved with foraging in the beach sand they do not look up. They depend on their noses almost to a fault to warn them of danger.

## REMAIN ALERT

As you get very close to a bear, remember how air movements can swirl. If you are within shooting distance, but trying to get closer, watch the bear carefully for any signs it has scented you. A bear that suddenly scents a human will stop, stiffen, straighten up, lift its head, sometimes stand up, maybe look in your direction, and often throw its nose in the air. Typically when any of these things happen, you will have two to five seconds before the bear is positive

*Remember this scene whenever you are stalking a bear. Wherever there is food, there may be dozens of bears in the area. In this scene, you can see them, but in most locations, the tall grass and brush can hide most, or all of them–until you stumble upon them at close range.*

about the source of the smell. Well over 90 percent of the time, the bear will suddenly race directly away from you, often right to the nearest cover. A small percentage of the time, perhaps when the bear is near its carcass mound, has cubs, or is with a sow in heat, the bear will immediately charge you. Either way, when you see signs a nearby bear has scented you, get ready to shoot–if you want to stop the bear.

You also need to remain alert to all your surroundings while on the stalk. Focus on the bear, but not so much you forget to watch for other bears. It is not unusual to spot or spook other bears while on a stalk. I once took a client just a short distance down from our spotting ridge into the bowl below us after a nearby bear. Before we had gone 800 yards, we spotted three or four (we weren't sure how many) more bears moving in the same bowl. We ended up shooting a different bear than our original target, and it may have been a half-foot smaller than the one we first stalked. Now I pay more attention to the surroundings during a stalk.

Just remember that we don't usually see most of the bears in any area. There is typically lots of brush, the bears are short and stick to cover, and our spotting knobs are not always ideal. There can be two or three times as many bears in our area as we see during an entire ten-day hunt. Remember to watch carefully for these other bears while you stalk one you have seen.

*Because bears ears and eyes aren't as acute as those of the game we typically hunt, and because bears sometimes sleep in unusual spots, we can literally walk right up on them. In these situations, you may only have seconds to judge the bear's size or its intentions. Prepare yourself by always remaining alert so you have a few extra seconds, and by learning to be a good bear judge (Chapter Nine, "Judging Bears").*

Stalking hunters need to be alert for another reason: some brown bears will stalk you. On one of my guiding trips, another guide from my camp and his client spotted a ten-foot bear high on a ridge in spring. While they were climbing to reach the bear, it apparently came down the mountain after them. The bear suddenly burst out of the alders at fifty yards coming right at them. Luckily, they saw the bear immediately and had their guns ready. The bear was relatively fat and had no obvious, painful injuries. It just decided to go after them for an unknown reason.

Another brown bear guide on Kodiak Island was stalked and mauled by a large bear just a few years ago. The guide saw the bear watching him through the brush and following along, but as an experienced guide, he thought the bear would just run off. The bear followed the guide a little and even got closer, but didn't act aggressively so the guide wasn't too concerned. By the time the guide realized the bear was going to charge, he didn't have time to get his gun up to shoot. The guide survived the mauling, but spent several months recuperating. The odds of this happening are very low, but hunters should always be very alert in brown bear country.

## RECOVERY AND REFUELING

I've often compared spot-and-run bear hunting to the way an African cheetah hunts. Out of necessity, cheetahs have to rest up between high-speed chases of their prey. Because these cats exert so much energy during a chase, they have to rest for hours before they are ready for another exhausting sprint after their supper.

Spot-and-stalk bear hunters often expend every bit of energy they have to cut off a moving bear. Sometimes you cannot catch the bear and sometimes you blow the stalk. Once you return to your spotting mound, you have to regain energy as quickly as possible to be ready for the next opportunity. To regain energy quickly, rest is vital, but so is food.

In the first two hours after any hard stalk, you need to drink lots of water to speed your muscles' recovery. Although carbohydrates are often promoted as the best food source for muscle recovery, a mixture of two parts carbohydrate and one part protein will replace your energy stores (in the form of muscle glycogen) faster. You need to begin this energy replacement as soon after a hard march as possible. If you don't get food within this "energy window" of two hours after hard exercise, your body will replace energy at only half the rate as that within the first two hours. The results will be that later that day and the next, you will have considerably less energy (glycogen) stored in your muscles when you need it. You will feel tired and weak.

To prepare for any times on a hunt when you are physically drained, bring along plenty of quick food that has a carbohydrate to protein ratio of about two or three to one. Candy bars will not do; they are mostly sugar and fat. Most of the energy bars will come close, and some of the protein bars will, too. You can always mix foods to get this ideal ratio. A protein bar eaten with some dried fruit or with an energy drink will usually fit this ideal ratio. Jerky with a bagel is also a good combination. Complex carbohydrates and complete proteins are the best choices at these times. (See my book *The Manual for Successful Hunters* for a complete explanation of nutrition for the hunter.)

Whatever you eat, doing so within the first two hours after hard exercise is vital, and the first twenty-five minutes is the best time to start. You should also remember this when you return to camp after a hard day, because dinner may take some time to prepare. Eat a snack of complex carbohydrates and protein right away to start fueling your body for the next day. By making a habit of replacing your energy stores quickly, you will be ready for the next opportunity or the next day.

Stalking bears can be an exhilarating experience. Planning and executing a successful stalk can tax the tactical abilities of even the most accomplished hunters, and on many stalks you will be physically taxed as well. Even if you can meet these mental and physical challenges of a complex, rigorous stalk, you are far from done with the hunt. Two very difficult tasks still lie ahead: judging the bear and shooting the bear.

*Getting close to bears is always a thrill, but it is not always a good thrill. These three large cubs are a perfect prescription for trouble. They are unpredictable, and wherever their mamma is, she is concerned for her cubs, and very unpredictable.*

*"You celebrate the victory, but you analyze the defeat."*
–Bill Walton

*The track of a Kodiak.*

# 9
# JUDGING BEARS

*"If you're going to think anyway, you might as well think big." –Donald Trump*

"Big" brown bears are what most hunters are looking for. However, the quality of an Alaskan brown bear trophy is dependent on several important characteristics. Trophies can vary in skull size, hair length, hair density, hair color, the number and severity of rubbed areas, age, and sex. Many of these variables can, to some extent, be predetermined by where and when you choose to hunt.

There is another variable—the difficulty of the hunt—which is seldom predetermined, but is perhaps the most important aspect of the hunt for many of us. Since memories are the real trophies we take with us after a hunt, the degree of difficulty we encounter, and overcome, can have the most significant influence on the intensity and vividness of these memories. Hunters who are prepared to overcome any difficulties of the hunt are more likely to carry home some incredible memories of hunting these noble creatures.

## BEAR SIZES

When comparing the sizes of brown bears, we judge them by both their hide size and their skull size. Their skull size is the sum of the overall length and the overall width, in inches. There is a Boone & Crockett official scoring form in the "Appendix" that explains in detail how to do this. The skull size of bears is used for record-keeping purposes

*The large ears, sitting on top rather than to the sides of the head, the smallish muzzle, the long legs, the large head in comparison to the body, and the small chest all indicate this is a small bear.*

because its measurements are consistent between any number of scorers. The size of a bear's hide is not used for record-keeping purposes because hides can be stretched considerably by hunters wanting to exaggerate the size of their bears.

Although there is a strong correlation between hide size and skull size, there are some variations in this relationship. Kodiak brown bears tend to have slightly larger skulls in relation to their bodies than Alaska Peninsula bears (I don't know why–probably some advantage for survival on Kodiak Island). I imagine there are other distinct populations of brown bears that also have tendencies for large or small skulls in relation to their hide size. However, estimating skull size in the field is virtually impossible. So, we estimate the hide size of a bear, which is much easier to do, and assume it will correlate pretty closely to the average skull size for that hide size.

The standard way to gauge a bear's size is to use its "squared" hide size. An eight-foot bear really means the "squared" size of the hide is eight feet. To get the "squared" hide size, the skinned and fleshed hide is laid out on a flat surface, fur side up. The width from the tip of one front claw to the tip of the opposite front claw is measured, and added to the length from the tip of the nose to the tip of the tail. This sum of the width and length is then divided by two. The result is the "squared" hide size.

The "squared" is usually dropped and bears are referred to as six, seven, eight (etc.) foot bears. Of course, hunters want to do their trophies justice, so you will here about eight-foot, six-inch bears, or nine-foot, three-inch bears. A ten-footer is considered the Holy Grail of brown bear hunting. I've heard some hunters claim they've seen eleven-foot bears or bear hides, but I have never seen one myself. One of the most difficult aspects of brown bear hunting is judging their size, but there are several reliable indicators to look for that simplify and make this task more accurate.

## JUDGING SIZE

Practice, practice, practice. There is no other way I know of to become a really good judge of bears. Take every opportunity to look at photos, look at bear mounts, watch videos, and talk to bear hunters about their methods of judging bears, as well as their successes and mistakes in this vital skill.

When you are practicing, these are the characteristics to look at when judging a brown bear's size:
• size of the head in proportion to the body;
• ear size and position;
• walking style – large bears waddle;
• leg length and thickness;
• chest size;

•hip size;

•and muzzle size.

All of these traits should be considered simultaneously. Bears are just like other animals; they have individual differences that may make it impossible to accurately judge their size based on just one of these traits. By using all of these criteria, a good bear judge can come up with a very accurate estimate of almost any bear's size.

*The first thing to notice about this bear is its large ears on top of its head. These indicate it is a small bear, as does the smallish muzzle and the relatively large size of the head compared to the body.*

The size of a bear's head in proportion to its body can be used at great distances to estimate size. This can save hunters a lot of wasted time going after distant bears only to find out they are too small. As brown (and grizzly) bears get larger, their head is smaller in proportion to their bodies. The term pinhead is often used to describe how a large bear looks. A seven-foot bear has already achieved about 70 percent of its head size, but its body can easily double or triple in overall mass, giving the head its pin-like appearance.

Small (young) bears have obviously large heads with relatively large eyes, just like young animals of any species of mammal. Small bears will also have relatively large ears that sit on top of their heads. The ears of large, mature bears will look smaller and less like they are on top of their heads, and more toward the sides of their heads. The ears on a two-hundred-pound brown bear are about the same size as the ears on a one-thousand-pound brown bear. Of course the head on the larger bear is almost twice that of the smaller bear, so the ears of the large bear look relatively tiny.

Many (but not all) large bears also have distinct muscle definition on top of their heads. Young bears will have no obvious muscle definition. Really large bears will also have necks as large around as their heads, whereas small bears will have obviously smaller necks than heads. Both of these criteria are less useful when hunting spring bears with long hair that disguises both muscle definition and true neck size.

Large bears tend to waddle as they walk. Very fat bears, even if they are medium size, may waddle also, but not to the same degree as large bears. Large bears waddle mainly because of the width of their shoulders and hips. Their legs seem to swing out and around their wide bodies with each long step so there is more side-to-side motion than smaller bears have. This motion also causes a large bear's head to sway from side to side as it walks, adding to the impression of a large, wide animal. Young bears have relatively long legs and narrow bodies; they walk more like dogs with legs that go directly forward and back with little side-to-side body or head movement.

*This is also a relatively small bear–as indicated by its prominent ears and large head. Its sloped brow and light color indicate it is probably a female.*

Young bears have relatively long, thin legs. This impression is enhanced by their small chests. I have seen young bears whose front elbows were both visible from a side view, and were way below their tiny chests. As a bear grows, its chest will expand downward, so it is level with or even below its front elbows. A brown bear's front (and back) legs also thicken considerably as its body gains mass, which also makes the legs look shorter. A young bear often has thin, dog-like front legs, adding to the impression that it is a young animal.

As most brown bears grow in size, their hips grow relatively faster than their shoulders, both upward and outward. Up to about seven or eight feet (in squared hide size) their shoulder width and height is about the same as their hip width and height. After this point, their shoulder growth slows down, while their hips continue to grow steadily–

outpacing shoulder growth. This produces the typical large bear shape of a wedge. Viewed from the side, the shoulders of many large bears are shorter than their hips. Viewed directly from the front, you can see their hips outside and above their shoulders. Viewed directly from the back, you will only see a large backside, as the hips extend above and outside of the shoulders, blocking the rest of the body from view.

The length and width of a brown bear's muzzle in relation to its head are also good clues as to its size. Basically, young bears have short, narrow muzzles; older (and larger) bears have longer, wider muzzles. The large snout of a nine- or ten-foot bear will make its eyes look tiny. A young bear appears to have much larger eyes in comparison to its snout. Large bears will have snouts that are almost half the length of the entire head. Young bears' snouts will be about one-third the length of their head length. The muzzles on some really large, old bears will widen to the point where their eyes are barely visible from a front view.

This next chart shows the (basic) relationships between the size of a skinned bear's hide (squared), the width of a front pad, the body weight, the width across the front paws, the length from nose to tail, skull size, and the shape of the front pads. Remember that individual differences, differences between populations, how deep an impression a track makes, whether a bear is fat in fall or thin in spring, how tight you stretch a hide, how old the bear is, and other variables may affect the relationships between these measurements in any one bear. However, if details from dozens of bears are recorded from one area, it is amazing how consistent, for example, track size is to hide size. Some veteran bear guides on the Kodiak Island or the Alaskan Peninsula can predict to within six inches (or less), the size of a bear's hide by seeing just one front track.

## Figure 9A.  SIZE RELATIONSHIPS

| squared hide size | 8-footer | 9-footer | 10-footer |
|---|---|---|---|
| front pad width in inches | 6-7 | 7-8 | 8-9 |
| body weight in pounds | 350-500 | 500-700 | 700-1,000 |
| distance across front paws, in feet | 9 | 10 | 11 |
| nose to tail distance, in feet | 7 | 8 | 9 |
| skull size, in inches | 22-24 | 25-27 | 26-29 |
| shape of front pad (right foot) |  ⬭ |  ⬭ |  ⬭ |

This chart is a good starting place for judging Alaskan brown bears. After looking at photos, bear mounts, and live bears, hunters should be able to determine if a bear in the field is small, medium, or large. After watching, estimating size, and then being in on several bear kills, hunters can hone their judging skills. The more characteristics on a bear that are used for judging, the more checks and balances a hunter has to avoid inaccurate size estimations.

On one of my spring guiding trips, my client and I watched a large, groggy bear slowly come our way. The client was adamant about wanting a bear over nine feet. I couldn't be sure of this bear's size because the head looked a little too big for the body, yet the body looked like a solid nine-foot bear. One minute he looked over nine feet, and the next I thought he was only eight and a half. The bear crossed a river right in front of us and I had to let it walk away upriver because I couldn't guarantee it was a nine-footer.

After the bear was out of sight, we hurried over to examine its tracks. The front tracks were at least eight inches wide. We had to hustle up the mountain, but about an hour later we caught that bear and my client got his nine-foot, three-inch trophy. When we reached the bear, I understood my estimation problems. The bear had a very furry, large head for its body, so the ratio of head size to body size seemed wrong for a nine-foot bear. The skull measured over 27 inches, which is on the large size for a nine-foot bear, but the track size (along with all the other nine-foot indicators) convinced me the bear was large enough for my client.

## SEX DETERMINATION

Determining sex on brown bears is possible with practice. I don't know if anyone can do this with 100 percent accuracy, but I do think 90 percent accuracy is quite possible. This task of distinguishing boars from sows is much easier when you are looking at large bears. It's the young bears and the small (but older) bears that are by far the most difficult to sex correctly.

The most common reason for wanting to identify male and female bears is for better game management. By shooting only male bears, bear populations are less affected by hunting pressure and more bears are available for hunting and for viewing. Most hunters want to help game managers for these reasons, but many hunters also prefer to take male bears because they feel it improves the trophy quality as well as increases the challenge.

There are several characteristics used to determine the sex of brown bears:
- the shape of the head;
- location of the ears;
- the length of the neck;
- the shape of the body;
- hair color;
- and body size.

Male brown bears have blockier heads than females. The male snout is almost square at the nostrils and the chin when viewed from the side. From a side view, females have more pointed noses, which makes the chin look more recessed. The same traits are apparent from a top view: a male's muzzle is square-looking, a female's is more pointed. From a front view, the male's face is also blockier; a female's is rounder. The ears of a male bear will tend to be more toward the side of the head than the top. A female's ears will appear to be more on top of its head.

### Figure 9B.  HEAD SHAPES

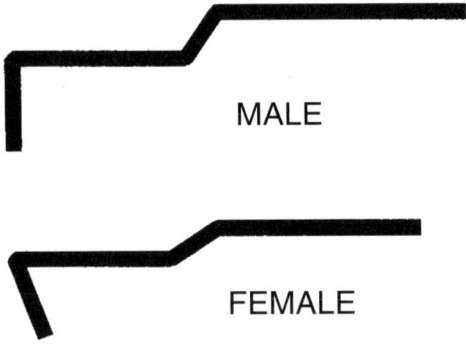

The ratio of neck length to head length for a male is between two-thirds and three-thirds. The same ratio for a female is less than two-thirds. For these comparisons, the length of the head is taken from the nose to the back of the skull. The length of the neck is taken from the back of the skull to the front of the hump. This is one of the most reliable predictors of sex in brown bears.

*The most reliable way to determine sex in brown bears is to compare the length of a line from the front of their hump to the back of their skull (#1 above) to the length of a line from the back of their skull to the end of their nose (#2 above). If #1 is 2/3 or more of the length of #2, it is a male. In this case, #1 is the same length as #2. This is a large boar.*
*The rule for judging males and females using neck length is:*
*The ratio of the length of the neck compared to the head length is:*
*Male = 2/3 to 3/3; Female < 2/3*

The shape of a male brown bear's body also differs from that of a female. Males have broader, squarer shoulders than females. When viewed from the front or the top, the shoulders of a male will be noticeably wider than its head. When viewing a female from the front or top, the shoulders will often look barely wider than the head.

When using the shape of the head, the ear position, the length of the head, or the shape of the body to determine sex, you must remember that all of these criteria are much more predictive with adult bears. Cubs of both sexes look quite similar because they don't typically display these sex-related characteristics until at least age three. These four predictive traits become even more pronounced as bears age, which is when these factors are most useful to hunters who are seeking only a larger, older trophy.

*The dark color, the large body, the big hips, the long neck, and the blocky head profile all indicate this is a large boar.*

Male brown bears tend to be darker than females. Blond bears are usually females, although a notable exception is the typical Toklat grizzlies, which in general have blond backs. Brown bears also tend to darken with age, so blond males will sometimes turn into dark adults, and even darker old bears. Very dark or even black-colored brown bears are almost always old bears.

Size is somewhat useful as an indicator of sex because boars get much larger than sows. Ninety-nine times out of one hundred, ten-foot bears are boars. Nine-foot bears are almost always boars. If you are hunting populations that seldom reach these proportions, size is not as predictive of sex.

As when you are estimating size, all the sex-determining traits should be used together to make your decision. Individual bears and populations differ, so no one sex-related trait can predict accurately throughout the range of brown bears in Alaska.

There is a good bear-judging video called *Take a Closer Look* that I recommend for all bear hunters. It covers most of the predictive criteria discussed in this chapter–both concerning size and sex. The video was produced at Alaska's McNeil River State Game Sanctuary. Copies of this video are available from the Yukon Fish & Game Association, 4061 Fourth Ave., Whitehorse, Yukon, CANADA, Y1A 1HT, 867-667-4263.

## OTHER TROPHY CONSIDERATIONS

In addition to helping determine sex of a brown bear, the color and hair condition of a bear can add or detract from its trophy quality. The Toklat coloration, with a blond back and very dark legs, was so named because of this classic coloration of many grizzlies coming from the Toklat region of Interior Alaska. However, this coloration can be found in bears throughout the state. Many of the larger boars in Alaska are dark-colored, so if hunters are mainly concerned with size, they have to take whatever color they get. Personally, I consider color and hair quality a more significant factor in trophy quality than many hunters do.

One of my fall, Alaska Peninsula hunters had two opportunities to take a beautiful, light-colored eight-footer, but passed both times to wait for a bigger bear. Although this was only an average-sized bear, its coloration was truly exceptional. When we first spotted this bear at about two miles, we both thought it was a caribou. It had its head up and stretched in the shape of a caribou, and it had a white mane and neck, just like a bull caribou. From the hump back, it was a perfect chocolate brown. I would have loved to take that bear myself, but the hunter insisted on trying to find a larger bear. We did find a larger bear, but I still wish he would have taken that bear with the white mane.

Just like other animals and people when they age, the older (and usually larger) bears often have ratty hair color and quality. The color will often be an inconsistent, dull, dark brown mixture, with no definite light or dark areas like a classic blond-on-top, dark-on-bottom Toklat. The hair texture will often be coarse, and there will be no colors at the tips that give many younger bears their attractive, grizzled look. Hair tips on old bears often seem to be broken and uneven, and the hair stands up at odd angles (just like an older hunter's hair).

On the other hand, many of us hunter-types (myself included) think that an old animal is more of a trophy and a better animal to harvest for management reasons. Male brown and grizzly bears often exceed the age of twenty years in the wild, and some sows have lived over thirty years. Older brown bears also tend to have white lateral lines on their claws, or even pure white claws, which adds to trophy quality. So there are both good and bad qualities you can find in older bears.

Rubbing of hides can be a significant concern for spring bear hunters. Bears rub in their dens and continue to rub once they emerge. Rubbed bears will have broken hairs that will be very short and unattractive. These shorter hairs are off-color from the surrounding hair, which still has its attractive, fine tips. Bears can rub and break their hair from just about anywhere on their bodies.

*Large bears make trails that have distinct left and right ruts, rather than just one wide rut through the grass. Their greater width results in a noticeable space between their left and right footprints.*

The parts of a bear to look for rubs are the forehead between the eyes, on the top of the rump right above the tail, on top of the paws, on the flanks in front of the back legs, and on the chest behind the front legs. As bears walk through crusty snow in spring, they can also break more hair from the top of their paws and from just about the entire length of their legs. Usually, any rubbed area can be identified by the discoloration, but a careful inspection with good optics is necessary to find all the rubbed areas.

A badly rubbed bear is a pretty disgusting sight. It will look like a vandal attacked it with an electric hair trimmer. Parts of the bear may even look like most of the hair has fallen out by the roots, leaving exposed skin. Close inspec-

*Whenever two bears are together, you must rule out the possibility of one being a cub. In this case, the smaller bear is light-colored, has a slender head, and looks like an adult. Also, the large bear is dark, huge, square-faced, and has a long neck, so he looks very male.*

tion of all parts of a bear's hide is crucial for hunters wishing to have a good, or even presentable hide to take home. Every spring I see some almost-bald bear hides taken by careless hunters–hides that are almost useless to anyone.

Judging bears is a vital skill for just about any bear hunter. It takes quite a bit of field practice to be very good, but adequate skill can be learned with some serious study of the criteria to use, and then some practice with photos, mounts, and videos. This will enable even the first-time bear hunter to judge between small, medium, and large bears in the field, as well as to identify the other characteristics that make a top-quality brown bear trophy.

*"My greatest trophies came when I worked the hardest and suffered what Hemingway called, '...the discomforts that you paid to make it real.'"* –Robert Ruark

# 10
# SHOOTING BEARS

*"Fear is just excitement in need of an attitude adjustment."* –Russ Quaglia and Doug Hall

My first experience with shooting brown bears came when I was ten years old. My father, my brother, and I had been flown into a mountainous area of Alaska to hunt caribou and moose. It was 1966 and game was plentiful, including bears.

We had camped next to a lake in a very brushy area with only a sheet of Visqueen for protection. We had brought fried chicken for dinner that first night and rose early the next morning to begin our hunt. We had been glassing only a few hours when here came a grizzly, no doubt wanting to share our chicken. My father immediately had us boys climb up a standing dead spruce tree to get out of reach of the bear.

When the bear again appeared through the brush, it was less than 100 yards away and still coming. My father didn't wait to see if he could scare the bear away, but just began shooting with his .300 H&H Magnum. The first shot dropped the bear, but it immediately regained its feet and was up and running. As the bear raced away through the brush, my father picked open spots in the brush to try and finish the wounded bear before it got away and became another hunting party's nightmare.

Each time my father fired, the bear went down, but quickly rolled to its feet and continued full-speed. When his gun was empty, my father reloaded and continued to fire. Finally, the bear stayed down after the sixth or seventh shot and rolled into the brush. We couldn't see the bear, but we thought it should be dead with all that lead it had absorbed. We watched for the telltale movement of brush, but it was suddenly very still after all the excitement.

*This bear was shot full of lead, but the hunters put one more into it just to make sure. After a few minutes of congratulations, they looked to find the bear had disappeared. Luckily, it was dead when they found it, but not before a few hair-raising minutes of following a wounded bear. Watch 'dead' bears until you are 100 percent sure.*

When my dad later checked on the bear, it had died right where we last spotted it. It was a relatively small grizzly, only about 300 pounds, but it took a lot of killing to die. That's my first and—after forty more years of bear encounters—my lasting impression of brown and grizzly bears: they are tough critters to kill.

In the past forty years, I have come up with these ba-sics for shooting brown bears:

- use at least a .30 caliber magnum cartridge;
- hit the chest area and try to break large bones;
- have a backup gun aimed before the first shot is fired;
- shoot the bear until it stops moving;
- definitely stop it before it reaches the alders or wil-lows;
- and keep your first shots under 200 yards.

There are a few exceptions to these rules, but in general, only experienced bear hunters should ever break this basic set of shooting rules.

## SIXTEEN REASONS TO KEEP SHOOTING

Compared to any other land mammal I have hunted, or have even heard or read about, a wounded brown bear will escape more often than any of them. Here are sixteen good reasons this occurs:

1.) Brown bears are tough to kill, particularly when their adrenaline is pumping after being shot.

2.) Their kill zone is proportionally smaller and far-ther forward than many animals, plus it is buried in-side a proportionally thicker animal than most horned or antlered game.

3.) They have thick, dense muscles and heavy bones that protect their (smaller) kill zones.

4.) They do not leave a good blood trail because their soft, fatty tissues (versus hard tallow of ungulates) plug entry/exit wounds and their dense, long hair absorbs a lot of blood before any hits the ground.

5.) Their kill zone is so low to the ground it is often obscured by even short vegetation or small undula-tions in the tundra.

6.) Bears are so short, it is often difficult to visually

track a running, wounded animal, and harder still to hit it.

7.) They live in brushy habitat and immediately go to the nearest, thickest cover, which they have pinpointed at any moment in their lives; they seldom have to hesitate to think which way to go.

8.) Bears can cause the most experienced hunters to get unnerved and shoot poorly.

9.) Many hunters over-gun themselves for bears and can't shoot their heavy calibers accurately.

10.) Bears have an extreme desire for self-preservation so they run very fast and very far when wounded.

11.) Some hunters are afraid to pursue wounded bears because bears will lie in ambush. As a result, some wounded bears are not followed into heavy cover when, in the same situation, experienced bear hunters or guides may have recovered them.

12.) Their soft pads don't leave as good a trail as sharp-hoofed ungulates would have.

13.) When bears die, no horns or antlers project upward to be seen by hunters in pursuit, plus their malleable bodies flow into any depressions, making dead bears difficult to locate.

14.) Their dead bodies will roll downhill amazing distances without leaving much of a trace; inexperienced hunters often don't realize this and lose animals this way.

15.) Because they have powerful front legs with sharp claws, they can pull themselves long distances into nearby brush and escape, only to die.

16.) Hunters are more experienced with wounded ungulates that typically choose somewhat visible spots to lie so they can see their pursuers. Hunters mistakenly expect the same tactic from bears. However, bears often choose very concealed hiding spots when fatally injured because they only need to smell or hear their pursuers, not see them.

Because brown bears are difficult to shoot accurately, kill quickly, track effectively, or find when they do get into brush, the standard practice of veteran bear hunters is to keep shooting until the bear stops moving. Many hunters lose bears because they do not follow this basic guideline.

*Even though this large boar is only in medium-height grass, he could disappear from view in less than one second if he moved into the taller grass. It only takes four feet, or less, of grass or brush to completely hide the largest bears. Once you start shooting, be prepared to keep shooting, or you may have to follow a wounded bear that you cannot see until you are within just a few feet.*

## CALIBERS & BULLETS FOR BEARS

Bullet placement is the number one factor in killing brown bears quickly and not losing wounded bears. To satisfy this requisite for effective shooting of bears, you must select a caliber and cartridge combination you shoot well.

This is the cardinal rule about weapon selection for all bear hunters.

The caliber you select (among those you can shoot well) for bear hunting is the second most crucial factor for quick, reliable kills. Considering the large size, toughness, and potential danger bears pose, the common recommendation is to choose the hardest-hitting caliber you can shoot accurately. I don't entirely agree with the first part of that advice. As long as you select a caliber that is within the acceptable range of brown bear calibers, there is no need to go to heavier calibers for that sake alone.

Almost every hunter's accuracy will suffer some as they climb the scale of heavy calibers, although they may still claim to be "accurate" shooters using them. Also, first-time brown bear hunters who buy a very heavy caliber just for a bear hunt, often don't have the experience with the new gun that they do with their weapons they have used for years. Accuracy on the range is one thing, but familiarity and confidence with a weapon is invaluable when the shooting starts. A hunter who has a familiar rifle in a satisfactory caliber for bear hunting, does not need to buy a new, heavier caliber rifle he has little confidence with. Most of the time, the familiarity with a tried and true rifle is much more valuable than a little extra firepower in a brand new gun.

I owned a .338 Winchester Magnum for about twenty years. I shot that rifle well from the first time I pulled the trigger. I took dozens of Alaskan game animals with it and had supreme confidence in my ability to hit what I aimed at. That was my backup rifle for ten years of brown bear guiding. A .338 Magnum is well within the acceptable range of brown bear calibers so I didn't need to replace it with an unfamiliar gun just for a bigger bear gun.

Once that .338 wore out (from too much rain, salt air, and abuse), I did replace it with a .416 Remington. Since I

*This would be no time to doubt your ability with your weapon. The cardinal rule about a bear weapon is that you shoot it well.*

had to replace the .338 with another backup rifle, I wanted to try this newer, heavier cartridge. I've only shot a few bears with the .416, but it does kill them well–if you hit them right. However, I am not nearly as accurate, confident, nor fast with the .416 as I was with my old, faithful .338. At best, my change to the heavier caliber was a wash. If given a choice, I would gladly take back the .338 if it was still as accurate as it used to be.

My recommendation for a suitable brown bear caliber is one that will send at least a 200-grain bullet out the muzzle at 2500 feet per second (fps). Those are not magic numbers so a caliber that comes really close is fine. But any caliber that is 10 percent deficient in either category—bullet weight or muzzle velocity—is a little too light for the average hunter. Of course, at higher velocities bullets are more likely to break apart before they penetrate sufficiently. So bullet construction becomes more important as velocities increase.

It is a well-known fact that the trusty .30-30 Winchester killed a lot of grizzlies throughout the continental United States in the early twentieth century. But just because a caliber can kill grizzlies (or brown bears), doesn't mean it is a wise choice for most hunters. Likewise, the .270 Winchester can kill the largest brown bears in the hands of a skilled, experienced bear hunter (or a lucky novice) if the shot placement is perfect, but it is far from the best choice for a brown bear caliber.

Using the 200/2500 rule, almost any .300 caliber magnum or larger is suitable. The 7mm Magnum is not. Nor is the .30.06, although it is a great caliber and has accounted for hundreds of brown and grizzly bears. Choose a caliber that meets the 200/2500 rule that you can shoot well, and if it is also flat-shooting, that is even better. The newer Remington Ultra Mags (I have a .300 Ultra Mag. that I love) and the Winchester Short Magnums are great examples of brown bear calibers that are also very flat-shooting. These are suitable calibers for use on virtually all big game in Alaska.

One full-time, Southeast Alaska brown bear guide uses a .300 Ultra Mag as his backup gun. He also uses it to lend to hunters whose guns fail or aren't suitable for the hunt. This guide shoots a lot more bears per year than I ever have, so this is a meaningful endorsement of this caliber. All the Remington Ultra Mags have tremendous knockdown energy, are very accurate right off the shelf, and are extremely flat-shooting. That is a hard-to-beat combination in any caliber.

There are several ways to improve your accuracy when shooting calibers heavy enough for use on brown bears. Muzzle brakes reduce recoil considerably as do some of the newer butt pads (I have a Decelerator pad on my new .300 Ultra Mag.). There are even easy-on and -off butt pads that reduce recoil by up to 70 percent. I use a six-inch square of Ensolite pad inside my jacket when range shooting, but there are commercial shoulder pads sold just for this purpose. Any combination of these add-ons you can use to further tame heavy calibers when range shooting will help prevent flinching, which is the main reason hunters don't shoot heavier calibers accurately. With this availability of numerous recoil-taming devices and competent gunsmiths to install them, there is no reason any adult hunter cannot shoot a suitable brown bear caliber accurately.

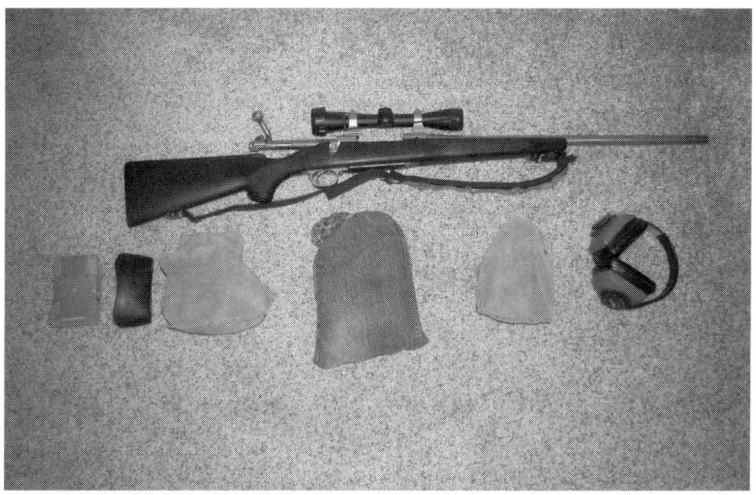

*I use a Decelerator pad, a doubled square of Ensolite pad, a soft rubber butt cup, two range sandbags, one handmade sandbag, shooting glasses (not shown), and earmuffs for range practice and to sight-in my rifle. The total cost of the range items is less than $100, but it prevents me from developing a flinch problem, my rifle is well-zeroed, and I shoot much better. There are ways to shoot even the magnums well (this is my .416 Remington).*

One very important consideration when selecting a suitable gun for bear hunting is the action. The only action strong enough to hold the pressures of brown-bear-sized calibers is a bolt action, but not all bolt actions are the same. Some of the heavy magnums are very tight and can't be worked as quickly as I would like. My .300 Ultra Mag. is like that so I can't feed shells nearly as fast as I could with my old .338. Some Mauser actions have a tendency to jam, which is not a good thing when bear hunting. Rifles also differ in the speed and reliability of their actions. Brown bear hunters should test calibers and rifles for both of these traits before selecting their bear gun. They can affect a hunter's success, health, and longevity.

Alaska brown bear hunting can turn wet and nasty at any time. Plus, a considerable amount of brown bear hunting occurs near salt water. Wet conditions are hard on guns, and moist, salty air is even harder on them. For these reasons, bear hunters often choose stainless or nickel-plated guns that corrode much slower than blued-metal guns. These more-resistant metals are just that, more resistant—not corrosion-proof. They will corrode much slower than a blued gun will rust, but they will still be affected by water or salt air so they must still be cared for.

Always have a good cleaning rod, patches, and plenty of rust protector on every bear hunt to protect your guns. Even a small, flexible rod will do if weight and space are limited on your hunt. Guns (made of any material) that are neglected in Alaskan brown bear hunting conditions will quickly show that neglect and may not function properly at the moment of truth.

For those experienced bear hunters who choose to use muzzleloaders for bears, Alaska requires you to use at least a .54 caliber or larger, or a .45 caliber with at least a 250-grain, elongated slug. There are not currently any restrictions on handgun use for brown bears. Both muzzleloaders and handgunners should have a reliable backup shooter ready to finish wounded bears. Neither muzzleloaders nor handguns (currently) meet my 200 grain, 2500 fps minimums, so experience and caution are both mandatory for

*Everything you do to prepare for an Alaskan brown bear hunt will affect the outcome. The weapon and the bullet are high-priority items you should select with great care and thought.*

anyone pursuing brown bears with either weapon. For bowhunting restrictions, see Chapter 11, "Bowhunting Bears."

The next consideration for shooting brown bears is bullet construction. If you have selected a bullet over 200 grains, that is flat-shooting through your rifle, and carries sufficient knockdown energy downrange, you must also select one that has good penetration on a large, tough Alaskan brown bear. A large percentage of the bullet must remain together no matter how many heavy bear bones it smashes through or how much distance it travels through a large bear. Most bullets made for non-dangerous game are not suitable for brown bear hunting.

Bullets that are suitable for brown bear hunting are Barnes X, Swift A-Frame, Nosler Partition, Winchester Fail-Safe, and Trophy Bonded Bear Claw (plus many custom bullets). Some of these can be quite expensive for target practice, but shooters can usually find a lower-cost alternative with the same point of impact to shoot while practicing. The more expensive bullets can then just be used as needed for final sighting-in, and then for the hunt. I personally used 210-grain, Nosler Partition bullets, factory loaded in Federal Premium ammunition for my .338 Win. Mag. with good results every time. Nosler Partition bullets are the least expensive, but suitable bullets I've found for bear hunting.

Rifle scopes for bear hunters don't need to be over four power because of the short-range shooting. There is nothing wrong with using a variable, as long as it can be set down to four power for close-range shooting. There is nothing worse than having an excited bear hunter who cannot find a bear in his scope because the field of view of his high-powered scope is too narrow. I've always used fixed scopes in four-power for bear hunting, and they have always been adequate.

For hunters whose eyesight is failing or for those unfortunate times when a wounded bear is over 200 yards away, a variable scope may be useful. Just remember to always keep your scope set down to no more than four-power while hunting, and only set it to a higher setting after the need arises. Higher magnification on a scope reduces the field of view, which is just what bear hunters don't want if a bear is suddenly spotted at close range.

Any rifle scope mounted on a heavy caliber bear gun has to be made to withstand the heavy recoil without falling apart inside. Low-cost brands will seldom qualify, but almost all the better scope makers will have models built tough enough to withstand the recoil of magnum rifles. Check out the manufacturer's claims, ask other hunters, and seek the advice of your local firearms dealers before you buy. I have had good luck with Leupold, Redfield, and even my upper-end Bausch & Lomb scopes on my bear rifles.

Any scope for Alaska brown bear hunting also has to be waterproof, not water-resistant. A fogged scope usually means the end of a bear hunt until it can be replaced. Even good scopes from high-end manufacturers can fog if they are not built to withstand the heavy recoil of the larger calibers. Repeated heavy recoil will ruin the moisture seal on all but the strongest scopes.

*A good scope will even reduce glare to manageable levels. The little details add up over the course of a hunt, or a hunting career, and result in a noticeable difference in success. Always buy good gear.*

Once you choose a suitable scope, you also have to mount it with solid rings and bases. Choose your mounting system with the same qualities in mind as with your scope— it must be tough enough to hold up to heavy magnum caliber recoil. Scope rings must be capable of tightening enough to prevent slippage of the scope. Any movement will cause your point of impact to change, possibly resulting in a wounded bear. Having a professional who is experienced with heavy magnum rifles mount your scope may be worth the minimal cost. Most gun shops will do this for free when you purchase either the weapon or the scope from them. Always watch carefully for scope slippage at the range before you go bear hunting.

Shooting sticks can be a great help in some bear-hunting situations. I have seen them used successfully on caribou and even tried them myself. They can really stabilize your rifle when you have to shoot from any position not providing a solid rest. Although it is always preferable to shoot bear with your gun resting on a solid, immovable object (like the earth), bear hunting involves brushy terrain and short animals—both of which can prevent finding a good rest that gives the hunter a clear view of his target.

Because bear hunting is often in brush and the animals are short, any suitable shooting sticks should extend up to 60 inches to allow for standing shots. The short bipods will not be usable much of the time because of the irregular, brushy habitat where brown bears live. Shooting sticks must also be light, fast to set up, and sturdy. I have seen shooting monopods, but the shooting (bipod) sticks will give the average bear hunter a much sturdier base to shoot from.

One mandatory rule for bear hunters is always zero your weapon again once you arrive at your destination. Taking a few minutes to shoot three or so rounds will confirm your weapon's accuracy and your confidence. At one of my bear camps, one scary client (luckily not mine) took just two shots at our field camp range. We spotted his two holes at 12 inches high and left, and six inches low and center. Then he proclaimed, "They're on the paper, that's good enough for me." His guide protested, but he put his rifle away and was ready to "...kill a bar."

I will even bore-sight my rifle at any time in the field if I have any doubts about its point of impact. There is no excuse for wounding bears and endangering hunters, guides and neighboring camps because a hunter is too lazy or too unskilled to properly sight-in his weapon. An accurate weapon is absolutely vital to the next step–shooting bears.

*Brown bears are often stalked, and then shot, in tall vegetation where there are no good rifle rests. Without a good rest, you must get even closer than might be possible. Shooting sticks can be a great aid in these (common) situations.*

## SHOOTING BEARS

Sounds simple, just point and shoot. For most non-dangerous game, it is almost that simple–find a good rest, aim, relax, squeeze the trigger, and go collect your trophy. Brown bears are different.

One authority on bear hunting claims that the average bear hunter is four times less accurate when shooting at a bear than when shooting on the range. That is a pretty scary statement considering the animal we are dealing with. One of the reasons Alaska requires nonresidents to hire a registered guide to hunt brown or grizzly bears is because inexperienced hunters (residents or nonresidents) just don't understand how to shoot these bears. First, you must have a good feel for how they react to being shot, or shot at.

*Two good reasons to learn the right way to shoot bears–they have large jaws and large teeth.*

Usually, brown bears run as fast as they can for the nearest cover when they hear a gunshot, whether they have been hit or not. With unalarmed bears, there is usually a one- to two-second delay between the shot and when they start running. If the bear is alert to the hunter's presence before the shot, it may be running in one-half second or less, and it may come after the hunter(s).

Even if a bear is shot through the heart and both lungs, it probably has from 30 to 60 seconds of oxygen available for its muscles and nervous system to function. Even 30 seconds is a long time–considering a bear can cover 100 yards in less than ten seconds. Even if you think the shot was perfect, it is very difficult to see exactly where the bullet hit and how it traveled through the bear. If you only hit one lung, the bear may live for hours or even days before dying. Once you have had to trail a wounded brown bear into the brush and find him still alive at close range, you will never want to do it again. Bears need more killing than most animals. There is a right way to do this, and many wrong ways.

Before shooting, the hunter and the backup gunner need to be 100 percent ready. This means their guns are in position and aimed at the spot on the bear they intend to hit. Ideally, both shooters are in a prone position and have solid rests. If prone positions are not possible, both shooters need to be in shooting positions they are confident with, given the range. Even for prone positions, perfect weather conditions, with a clear shot at a perfectly still, broadside bear, the maximum range for shooting brown bears should be limited to 200 yards. For many hunters with less skill and experience, that range should be less than 100 yards.

There are plenty of experienced hunters who can shoot their heavy, magnum calibers very accurately out to 300 yards or more, and can remain calm enough to do this when the target is a brown bear. However, the concern is not just hitting the kill zone with the first shot, it is those follow-up shots that are so difficult on now-moving bears. Even if the bear goes down and is just rolling around, as they often do, at ranges of even 100 yards it is very hard to identify which part of the bear is visible. Unlike game animals most of us are used to shooting, bears do not collapse straight down, get their feet back under them, and then stand straight up. When bears are knocked down by bullets, their movements are much more comparable to that of a wrestler. Their heads tuck, they roll, they bite at the bullet entry point, they roar, they may spin around on and off their feet several times, and then they may suddenly be running full bore just like they are unhurt.

Even if you are within 100 yards of a bear reacting from a shot, you may only see a blur of fur with occasional, brief glimpses of various body parts. If you are 200 yards away or farther, it will certainly be just a blob of animal with no apparent up or down, right or left. Then the blob may suddenly disappear into a slight depression in the earth you would swear wasn't there before you shot. You will be sitting there, nervously hoping the bear rolled over and died just a few feet from where you last saw it. A few, short seconds later you may catch a glimpse of motion out of the corner of your eye, and turn to watch in horror as your "dead" bear speeds toward the sanctuary of the nearest brush, disappearing again before you can get off another shot.

Or, perhaps you won't even get a glimpse of the bear because it will find a slight trough in the tundra and run along it right into the brush where it feels most at home. The reason to limit how far we shoot at brown bears is not because we aren't skilled enough to send bullets through their kill zones at long ranges, it is because of the aftermath of the first shot, when many of the sixteen reasons I listed at the beginning of this chapter come into play. Hunters need good, short-range opportunities to put second, third and fourth shots into bears so they do not escape to either die where they can't find them or to force them to follow wounded bears into the brush. Neither of these possibilities are acceptable for sane, ethical hunters. Bears simply need to be shot in a different manner than most hunters are used to.

Before the first shot is fired, but after both the hunter and the backup gun are aimed and both are ready to fire, the hunter must be able to pinpoint the right aiming point on the bear. At this point, both gunners need to know a good deal about bear anatomy and where they should place bullets. The first shot should (almost) always go through the heart/lung kill zone. The exceptions to this would be when a bear appears at close range either charging the hunters or about to charge. In these cases, the animal may need to be slowed or stopped first by breaking large bones in the shoulders, upper legs or the spine or maybe even shot through the brain.

Figure 10A.  BEAR ANATOMY

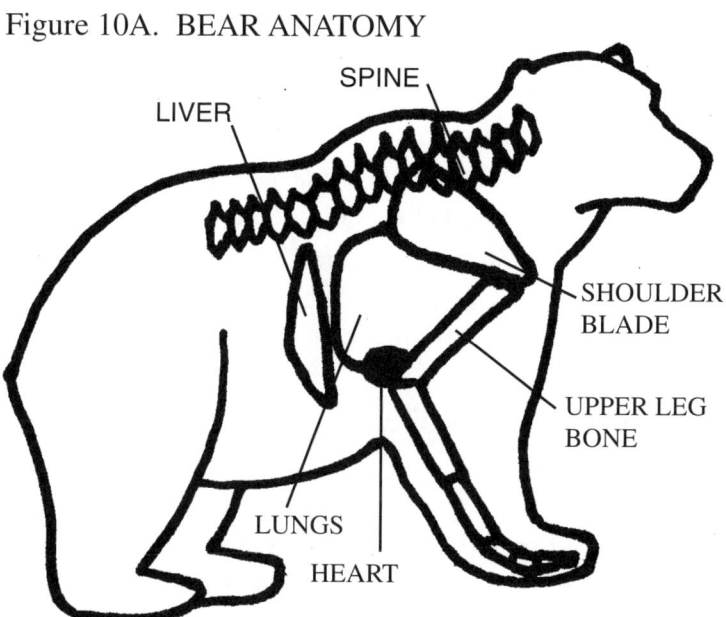

*These are the basic parts of a bear's anatomy of which you should know the locations. The spine is a small target and so is the heart. The lungs are the largest organ to shoot for that will kill the animal quickly. The upper leg bone and its joint with the shoulder blade are the two spots to try to hit when you hit the lungs. These bones are not large, but they are the bones you are most likely to break as you hit the lungs, depending on the bear's position and your shot angle.*

When the standard kill-zone shots are taken on bears, the shooter(s) should also take out large shoulder or leg bones, or try to break the spine. The highest priority should be to put a killing shot into the bear by sending the first shot through its vital organs; the next priority is to break some large bones that will slow it down or stop the bear completely. In order to do this consistently, you must know the anatomy of a brown bear from all angles. Studying the illustrations and photos in this chapter, and book, is a good start, but you should also study the anatomy of any bears you get a chance to skin.

Whichever angle you are shooting from, you must visualize the location of the major bones and the heart/lung kill zone. This is quite different from looking at a paper target of a broadside bear with its skeletal system and vital organs drawn in. A live bear is three dimensional so you have to factor in the thickness of each bear you are shooting at. Every little twist, lift, step, bend, or crouch a bear makes will affect the alignment of the bones and vital organs. The better a hunter is at visualizing how any movement will alter his best point of aim, the better shooter of bears that hunter will be.

The ideal shot placement on a perfectly broadside bear is to break the near joint of the upper (front) leg bone where it meets the scapula. The bullet path should continue through both lungs, and then the bullet can also take out the same upper leg bone/scapula joint on the far side of the bear. This shot placement will break both shoulders of the bear so it cannot run, plus it will die in less than 60 seconds. When trying to accomplish this ideal shot placement, or any other first shot, the first priority is to always go through the heart/lungs so the bear will be dead shortly. Breaking bones prevents the bear from moving fast, but is secondary to the need to make a killing shot.

*This bear has its near (front) leg forward and its far (front) leg back a little. The best aiming spot would be at the white circle. A bullet placed here should go through both lungs and may break the upper leg bone on the far leg. When shooting at bears, just imagine where each front, upper leg bone is and try to hit one of them, as well as the lungs.*

It is common for hunters to become excited and start shaking when they are about to shoot their first brown bear. If this happens, they must wait until they can hold steady for the first, crucial shot. Sometimes bear hunters will have to wait hours for a sleeping bear or a bear on a carcass to get up and present a good shot angle. It is often very difficult to even ascertain what body part you are looking at on lying bears. Hunters must have the patience and nerves to wait for the right shot. They must be alert and ready to shoot for as long as that takes, because a sleeping bear may suddenly get up and move. Hunters may only have a few seconds when the right shot presents itself, before the bear begins moving too fast to shoot, out of sight into the brush, or behind some obstacle.

The second shot is when most inexperienced bear hunters make their biggest mistakes. Even the calmest, surest shooters may not hit any bones with their first shot, even though they do score a direct hit through the heart/lung area. As I said earlier, a bear with a killing shot through this heart/ lung zone can still run for up to 60 seconds, which is more than enough time to reach any nearby brush and disappear. Even if the bear dies quickly, it may be difficult or impossible to find the animal–due to any of the "Sixteen Reasons" listed earlier in this chapter. If shot at close range, the bear may also charge the hunters with enough life left to do considerable damage. Of course, since the exact shot placement cannot be discerned with absolute certainty, the bear may be very much alive and able to live for hours or days. There are so many uncertainties when shooting these dangerous animals, that making quick, well-placed second and successive shots is the only practical way to kill them with any certainty.

I tell my brown bear hunters that after they shoot and I am positive they have hit the bear, there are three scenarios:

1.) the bear collapses and stops moving completely or almost completely to my satisfaction, in which case I will not shoot;

2.) the bear is still in motion, either in one spot or moving away, and within one second of their first shot, the hunter continues to shoot and hit the bear until it is no longer moving or even quivering–in which case I may not have to shoot;

3.) or the bear is still in motion, and one second has elapsed, in which case I will shoot (and reload and continue shooting, if that is necessary) until the bear stops all movement.

Once a bear has been shot, it becomes adrenaline-charged and can do amazing things, one of which is to take a lot of lead and keep going (or coming at you). The second shot has to hit the bear before it has the opportunity to begin running. A running bear, even at close range—let alone at a hundred yards or more—is very difficult to hit with any reliability, even by a skilled shooter on the best of days. Even a bear that seems to be down and maybe out, cannot be trusted to stay down. Half of the brown bears I've seen shot, or heard stories about, fall to the ground immediately, but get back up and run–unless well-placed, follow-up shots are fired within a few seconds. Brown bears that have been hit, but are still moving, should be shot again and again until they stop moving–that is how to shoot brown bears.

*This Talkeetna brown bear (I consider it a mountain grizzly) was hit hard three times, but was still able to go about 100 feet into the brush. It had the typical Toklat coloring.*

The story about my first experience with shooting brown bears that begins this chapter is a classic example why bears must usually be shot repeatedly. After it had been hit the first time, that bear hit the ground at every shot my father fired, whether it was hit or not. Examination of the bear showed it had only been hit with about half of the bullets that were fired, but it still fell immediately as if it were down for the count–only to quickly roll to its feet and continue running at full speed. Anytime a wounded bear is running toward or in thick brush, the odds of recovering that bear have dropped to about 50 percent. Those are terrible odds and ethical hunters (or those who honestly want that bear) shouldn't let that happen. Quick follow-up shooting until the bear stops moving is the best way to prevent this from happening and collect the trophy.

Among the established bear guides in Alaska, there are two schools of thought. One approach (the one I consider the best one) assumes there will be no one-shot kills on brown bears. Once the client hits the bear, the guide will help the client shoot it until it is dead. The rare exceptions are if the guide can't get a shot into the bear, or the bear is obviously dead to both hunters' complete satisfaction–any doubts and more shots will be fired into the bear. The reasoning behind this, in addition to my "Sixteen Reasons" plus everything I've explained about bear shooting, are that ammo is cheap and replaceable; people are not. Following a wounded brown bear puts the client's and the guide's lives at unacceptable risk. Hunting brown bears is slightly dangerous given this approach to shooting them; hunting brown bears with any other approach is unnecessarily dangerous for the hunters, and will lead to an unacceptable number of wounded and/or lost, and wasted, bears.

The other school of thought a few of the older guide camps still cling to is that the guides will not shoot unless it is absolutely necessary to prevent a wounded animal from escaping. (Some guides even think it is unethical for them to shoot a client's wounded bear, except to save lives.) This approach assumes a guide has the ability to wait until the

*This is a difficult angle at which to shoot a bear with any certainty. You might aim for the spine, but you may ruin the skull that way. And if you hit to the side at all, you will miss the spine and only wound the animal. It would be best to wait for this bear to turn at least a quarter to one side so the head is not blocking the kill zone.*

last moment possible, when a wounded bear is just about to get away, and will still be able to stop the bear with any certainty. Wounded bears that are traveling at full speed often need four, five, or more good shots to stop, more than the majority of guides can place into a running bear even if their rifles did carry that many cartridges in their magazines.

A hunter and I once placed eight good shots from our magnum rifles into a large brownie, although he was hit hard and dropped immediately after the first shot. As we were reloading, somehow he was able to crawl up a fifteen-foot embankment and disappear into the brush–while I was emptying my gun for the second time into the fully exposed backside of the bear. The client assumed the bear was dead, and hadn't reloaded, to our dismay. The bear died several minutes later, but not before it traveled fifty yards into the dense brush, where we couldn't see it.

Another time, we set up near an open-tundra trail waiting for a large bear to walk by. We had perfect rests, and my hunter was an older, accomplished big-bore, competitive shooter who was absolutely cool during all phases of the hunting and shooting of this bear. The bear dropped immediately from the client's .375 caliber bullet at 100 yards. I had instructed the client about my one-second rule, and he seemed to understand. However, when the bear went down, but continued to roll around and spin, the client calmly, and slowly ejected the spent shell, and slowly reloaded another.

Because of what I had observed and heard over the first six days with this client, I was sure he would shoot the bear as I had instructed. So, I was a little too slow to pick up on what was happening. I was in a sitting position with my rifle resting firmly across my knees, just like the client only a few feet away. I had my sights on the bear, a .338 round chambered, my safety was off, and my finger was touching the trigger–exactly how a brown bear backup gunner should be.

When the ten-footer went down, but kept moving, I knew in my mind the client would simply shoot successive, well-paced shots until the bear was dead. I waited, but no more shots rang out. Sighting down my rifle, I could only see the client's feet with my peripheral vision. At that point, I wondered if his gun had jammed or something worse had happened. I took my eyes off the bear for one instant to check on the client, only to see he was slowly reloading like he was at a range and wanted the gun to cool a little between shots.

*This is not a bad angle at which to shoot a bear. Aim at the white circle and you will hit the lungs and maybe the far, upper leg bone.*

I immediately snapped back to my rifle to sight in on the wounded bear, only to see him disappearing into the tundra. I quickly fired two shots into the bear's visible backside as it went entirely out of sight. We were perched on the side of a slight mound and about ten feet higher than the bear trail. There were only a few, tiny scattered clumps of brush within several hundred yards of us or the bear trail, so I had not been worried about the bear reaching any cover quickly. To my amazement, as I later discovered, right next to, and paralleling the bear trail was a four-foot trough running for hundreds of yards over the tundra–plenty deep enough to hide a wounded, running bear.

Luckily for us, the bear expired just a few feet away from where we last saw it. However, as the client and I sat on that mound anxiously watching in all directions for any sign of his wounded bear, I feared for the worse and thought

*This eight-foot sow is one of only two brown bear kills I've been in on that ended after just one shot. My hunter was about 30 yards away and out of sight when the bear appeared. He shot it once. By the time I arrived, it was obviously dead.*

we might never see my client's huge trophy bear again. We stayed put for several minutes so we could make the best use of our eyes and not be distracted while walking toward the bear trail. We could have lost that bear in the two seconds I wasted checking on my hunter. Two seconds would have been plenty of time for the bear to get into that trough and out of sight. It could have run along that trough, out of sight until it reached brush or been too far out for us to hit while it was running at full speed. I've seen several bears disappear, only to reappear running at top speed just a few anxious seconds later, and they quickly get too far out to hit with any certainty.

I've only seen one first-time brown bear hunter that did what I instructed when shooting his first brown bear. That was a Canadian guide who had guided hundreds of black bear hunters, so he had a decent understanding of bears. I had traded a brown bear hunt to this Canadian guide (for several of his whitetail hunts) so he could hunt these remarkable animals. He kept shooting as I instructed, and five shots later the eight-foot, six-inch Kodiak bear finally stopped quivering–after moving fifty yards from the point of the first (probably lethal) shot. Other than this bear guide, I've never had any hunter who fired a second shot quickly enough to suit me. Of all my other bear hunters whom I've been right next to when they fired, I've always had to shoot at the bear myself to guarantee it didn't escape.

The "no one-shot bears" approach is safer, more humane, and more practical for shooting brown bears. The "don't shoot your client's bear" approach is more egotistical, much more dangerous, and less respectful of the animal. They deserve to die quickly. They should not be wasted when this approach results in wounded bears that get away, and some will get away. The farthest any of my twenty-some brown bear kills have made it into the brush was the one I just wrote about a few pages ago–fifty yards into the brush with eight shots in the bear.

The last aspect of shooting bears to learn is how to approach a "dead" bear. At least one of the shooters should be able to watch the bear at all times during the approach. If necessary, one shooter waits where he can see the bear, while the other shooter goes ahead until he can again see the bear. The waiting hunter should also be able to see the approaching shooter at all times, if possible. If the cover is so thick an approaching shooter will not be able to see the bear until he is very close, the waiting shooter may have to stay on a lookout point where he can see both the approaching shooter and the bear. When the approaching shooter again can see the nearby bear, the waiting shooter should come up to join him.

For the final approach (the distance will depend on the visibility), the two shooters should ideally go in side by side to about thirty feet. While one shooter waits there with a round in the chamber and his finger on the trigger, the other shooter should move in to be certain the bear is dead. Always approach a "dead" bear from its rear. I like to toss a stick or rock at the bear first and watch for any response, and then go up and poke it in the backside with the barrel of my loaded rifle and my finger on the trigger.

The waiting shooter must be positioned so he will have a clear shot at the bear at all times and not be blocked by the approaching shooter. If there is any doubt that the bear is dead, it is very cheap and quick to put another round into the bear. The hole can easily be sewn up by a taxidermist (don't hit the skull) and it is a small price to pay for insurance the bear is dead. Likewise, if the bear is positioned so that the approaching shooters won't be able to keep it in sight easily, they can stop and simply put another round into the carcass from where it is last visible. As long as these insurance shots are kept away from the head, there should be no damage to the trophy whatsoever.

I heard one story about a guide that had his client shoot a bear that came into camp, and then didn't put any insurance rounds into the bear–assuming it was dead. They put their guns down before checking the bear, and several minutes later it came to life and charged. They survived, but risked their lives unnecessarily for want of a couple dollars worth of ammo.

*This is another okay shot angle, but not the best. Aim at the white spot and you could hit the spine and the bear would be dead immediately. If you hit high, but centered, you could also hit the spine. If you miss slightly to either side of the white spot, you could still get one lung and maybe a shoulder blade. However, if you hit too low, you may kill the bear, but ruin the skull. This angle and aiming point allow for a lot of possibilities, but you could still kill the bear quickly–just plan on firing well-placed, follow-up shots immediately. Unless you are close or a very good, cool shooter, you should wait for a broadside or quartering shot angle for the best odds.*

In summary, the best way to shoot brown bears to produce consistent, reliable, humane kills, and to keep to an absolute minimum the number of wounded bears who get away or endanger human lives is:

1.) all shooters (at least two) should be in stable shooting positions;

2.) all guns should be aimed, rounds chambered, safeties off, and trigger fingers in place;

3.) the bear must be at a proper angle so its vital organs are visible to both shooters;

4.) the bear must not be behind brush or even heavy grass that will deflect the bullets;

5.) the first shot placement must be through vital organs and whenever possible, through heavy bones of the shoulder, front legs, or spine;

6.) follow-up shots should start immediately unless the bear is down and not moving;

7.) follow-up shots should continue until the bear is unquestionably dead, and then shooters need to remain focused on the bear for at least another full minute to watch for signs of life;

8.) as shooters approach the bear they need to remain alert the entire time–it is best for at least one shooter to keep the bear in sight for the entire approach, until they reach the bear and are certain it is dead;

9.) and additional shots into "dead" bears are cheap insurance you and your buddy will live to hunt again.

## AFTER THE SHOT

Despite following all the right rules about shooting bears, hunting bears is unpredictable so even veteran hunters may still end up with a wounded brown bear in the brush. The odds of finding a wounded bear and doing it safely depend on what the hunters do from the moment they shoot the bear.

First, always watch carefully for a bear's reaction to the shot. This is a crucial job of the backup shooter. He needs to be positioned so the muzzle blast from the first

*Bears look so docile and slow before the shooting starts, but you must always be alert to what will happen when the first shot is fired. If she is able, this small sow will immediately run as fast as she can for the nearest cover–in this case, the tall grass that is only a few feet away.*

shot does not interfere with this most important job. Like any animal, bears will usually react according to where they have been hit. Flesh wounds may momentarily drop them, or they may barely flinch and immediately break into a run. Shots that break bones will almost always drop them for at least an instant. Broken leg bones will usually slow them down, but not too much in some cases. A three-legged bear can often outrun a hunter with ease.

Whenever you shoot a bear on a slope, there is the possibility the body will roll, and on a steep slope, bear bodies can roll as fast as the bear could have run down the slope. Rolling bears are almost always dead bears if their legs and neck are completely relaxed and flopping as they roll. They roll down steep hills so fast, it is very difficult to hit them. They can also slide down snowy slopes too fast for most hunters (myself included) to hit them. I've had several slide right by me at amazing speed. Remember this

*We shot this Kodiak bear when it was perched on a steep hillside, sleeping on a snow patch. The first shot dislodged the bear from its bed and we could only get in two more shots before it slid out of sight. It slid and rolled over 100 yards downhill through heavy brush, where we were relieved to find it–very dead.*

if you ever shoot at a bear that is uphill from you. The bear— alive or dead—is likely to be in your lap in a hurry. If possible, don't shoot bears directly uphill from you for this reason.

If you shoot a bear near water, be prepared to move as fast as you can to the bear. Typically, they will slowly sink. You may have a few minutes at most before the bear sinks out of sight and is gone. Bears have solid hair, not hollow hair like ungulates, so no air is trapped inside their hair to float their dead bodies. Because of this, you need to think ahead when you are about to shoot a bear near water or on the beach. Alaska's extreme tides can quickly claim a dead bear on a beach that is not attended to immediately.

If a wounded bear is out of sight or out of range and getting away, and has to be tracked, this is the procedure to follow:

1.) watch the bear's route as long as it is visible, even if you can only see the brush move occasionally as the bear plows through it–this may make the difference between finding and losing the bear;

2.) wait one full hour before trailing the bear;

3.) if you lose sight of the bear, start watching all directions and distances even if you think the hit was perfect–they are amazingly tough and, once their adrenaline is up, will run miles with what should have been a mortal wound;

4.) always trail in groups of two or more shooters;

5.) never trail a bear in the dark;

6.) if you wait for over an hour or overnight, always look for birds on or hovering over the dead bear;

7.) mark the trail as you follow it with squares of tissue paper (highly visible and biodegradable if you can't pick them all up afterward);

8.) the lead shooter should look ahead, on the ground, and on short vegetation for sign of the bear's trail while the backup shooter(s) covers him, preferably following the tracker slightly behind and to one side to always have a clear shot–two followers flanking one tracker are better than only one follower;

9.) do not talk while you track unless absolutely necessary, work out hand signals so your voices don't spook a wounded bear before you get close enough to finish it;

10.) watch your paper trail for a pattern in the bear's route, mortally wounded bears will sometimes circle back on their trail in a "J" pattern and lie in wait for following hunters, but they may also die along the "J" route and be impossible to spot if you are not watching carefully;

11.) profuse bleeding at first, which then slows or stops without the bear lying down, means it was probably not a heart or lung wound–more likely a leg wound– and the bear will be very alive and alert if you can find it;

12.) a bear that lies down in the first 100 to 300 yards was probably hit hard and has a serious or fatal wound;

13.) note how high on the brush you find blood to identify where the wound is;

14.) bright red, bubbly blood is a lung hit, darker blood is a muscle or liver wound;

15.) a liver-shot bear will die in three to six hours, an intestinal or stomach-shot bear will take one to three days to die;

16.) and if you lose the trail, start at the last definite sign and make 180 degree arcs ahead in the direction the trail was heading in five-yard intervals until you rediscover the bear's trail, but be alert because when you are focusing on the ground you are not watching for a bear waiting in ambush for its pursuers.

If you never have a need for this list, at least reading it should convince you that my "no one-shot bears" approach is a pretty good idea. Shooting at these inspiring, remarkable, beautiful, and dangerous creatures is more exciting and unnerving than most any other creature we hunt. Scores of experienced hunters have taken short-range shots at Alaska's giant bears and missed–repeatedly. The closer the shots, the more some hunters seem to miss.

On one of my personal Kodiak adventures to bowhunt Sitka blacktail deer, two members of my group were rifle hunting for Kodiak bears. One day I came upon them waiting for a large, unalerted Kodiak brown bear to stand up and give them a clear shot. When the bear finally stood up, these two experienced Alaskan hunters shot the bear in the

*Taking a good Kodiak brown bear, as this hunter has, is a dream of many bear hunters.*

foot at about 125 yards. The slightly wounded bear began loping in their direction, not knowing where his assailants were. They both emptied their guns without touching the bear again. As much as I wanted to, I couldn't help because I only had my bow. The bear's very skimpy blood trail led up the valley for a few miles and then up and over a 3,000-foot mountain. I couldn't believe these two hunters couldn't hit this huge bear as it loped broadside in front of them at less than 80 yards.

One of my fellow guides tells about one of his clients that took several shots from 20 yards to 120 yards at four different, stationary bears, and never touched one during a ten-day hunt. Bears do that to even veteran hunters, time and time again. Bear shooting is not as simple as point and shoot. They are a great animal to hunt, but you need exceptional shooting rules and the discipline to follow them to kill these creatures quickly and reliably. Shooting Alaskan brown bears is no simple feat; it is a challenge that should not be taken lightly.

*Shooting well is doubly important for bowhunters. This bowhunter has taken a ten-foot Kodiak bear–perhaps the most difficult challenge for a bear hunter.*

*"To fear is one thing. To let fear grab you by the tail and swing you around is another."* –Katherine Paterson

# 11
# BOWHUNTING BEARS

*"To be tested is good. The challenged life may be the best therapist."* –Gail Sheehy

Most hunters would agree that bowhunting for Alaskan brown bears is a challenge. Those hunters and guides who have considerable experience with these powerful, unpredictable creatures would more likely say that it is a tremendous challenge. As of this writing, there are several dozen bowhunters who have met this tremendous challenge successfully. There are also a couple women bowhunters who have recently accomplished this.

Bowhunters who are considering this challenge must realize that it will probably take several hunts, over several seasons, to accomplish this task. Seldom does a bowhunter succeed during his first hunt. Those that do are very lucky, very good, have a very good guide, or have all three of these factors going for them. Bowhunting Alaska's brown bears is not for neophytes or casual hunters; it should only be attempted by experienced bowhunters, with either a good understanding of bear hunting themselves or with the help of an exceptional bear guide.

## ALASKA'S BOWHUNTING LAWS
Alaska has equipment regulations that are specific for bowhunting brown and grizzly bears. Currently, these regulations are:

•the bow must have a peak draw weight of at least 50 pounds;

•the arrow must be tipped with a broadhead, at least 20 inches in overall length, and 300 grains in total weight;

•the broadhead must be a fixed or replaceable-blade type broadhead–mechanical/retractable-blade type broadheads are not permitted for brown or grizzly bear hunting;

•and the broadhead cannot be barbed.

One of the concerns these equipment restrictions address is achieving sufficient penetration on these large, tough animals. There are many bowhunters who think using a heavy arrow, a higher draw-weight bow, and a two-bladed broadhead will improve their ability to kill a bear quickly. The combination of razor-sharp, two-bladed broadheads and heavy arrows may improve penetration slightly, but unless you also increase the poundage of the bow, the killing effectiveness is probably no better than using a three-bladed broadhead that may not penetrate quite as much, but makes up for that by cutting a wider wound channel through the bear.

I know of several brown bears that have been successfully taken with three-bladed, replaceable-blade broadheads. Heavier draw-weight bows will help some, but not if you have to sacrifice placement or the ability to draw the bow quickly and hold it steady. The minimum-draw-weight bows and minimum-weight arrows will kill brown bears just fine with one well-placed arrow.

## HUNTING METHODS

The basic hunting methods described in Chapter Seven "Hunting Bears," can all be used by bowhunters pursuing brown bears. All of the general principles apply to bowhunting with the usual caveats about the short ranges necessary

*This large grizzly was taken north of Galena. There are minimums for archery gear used to take these bears–for good reasons.*

for bowhunting. However, there are several important factors bowhunters should recognize to increase their odds of success.

Most bowhunters targeting brown or grizzly bears choose fall bear season rather than spring. In fall, bears can be found on food sources that will slow them down and keep their attention focused downward. Bears grazing on dense berry crops or fishing for salmon in fall tend to be less alert to a nearby bowhunter. Spring bears tend to wander much of the time so their movements are difficult to predict.

However, it is easier to find the really large bears during daylight hours in spring, and they can be groggy (and more stalkable) immediately after coming out of their dens. In fact, several of the largest bears taken by bowhunters were hunted in spring. Bowhunters will find more good opportunities for success in fall, but for those who are looking for a really large bear, spring may be a better choice.

*Salmon streams are great places for bowhunters to get close to brown bears. Some bowhunters prefer to be in an elevated stand when shooting these bears; this hunter is on the ground and only 30 short yards from the bear.*

Salmon streams are by far the single most popular place for bowhunters to pursue brown bears in fall. Bowhunters can walk salmon streams, sit on high banks, or sit in tree stands overlooking prime fishing spots. Bears often won't look up for several minutes or more as they walk along or in a stream intent on catching their next meal. The most critical factor is determining wind direction plus any variations that will carry scent to bears. Bowhunters must constantly monitor air movements even more than firearms hunters. A bowhunter should have a powder bottle to detect the slightest wind currents that may carry human scent to a bear.

Tree stands used to hunt over salmon streams must be placed with the utmost care to avoid scent contamination of the area before or while hunting. The first priority is to find a good location. Most promising stand locations for rifle hunters will not do for bowhunters pursuing brown bears for several reasons.

Bowhunters' tree stands must almost always be right on the streamside to afford a good shot opportunity. Most of the streamside locations with good bear sign, good visibility, and a suitable tree will have unpredictable wind currents. A suitable location will have a predictable wind direction, even if it is only during morning or evening. This will allow the bowhunter to get to the stand as well as hunt it for at least one time period (morning or evening) without spooking bears.

A suitable stand will also allow for the bowhunter to approach and exit the stand without spooking bears. Both a predictable wind direction and a good travel route are often afforded by a significant feature in the terrain. A high bluff, a dense stand of trees, or a body of water may suffice to funnel wind one way and provide noise and visual cover. Before the hunt, the approach route can also be raked to remove leaves, twigs, and other noisy items from the trail. Pruning shears can be used to cut any bothersome limbs that will alert bears to your approach to a stand.

Some streams with huntable bear populations are just too brushy to be hunted successfully on foot. We once took a nice brown bear by anchoring in the middle of a large stream and waiting for the bear to come out of the dense brush to fish. Bears seldom expect danger on the river and will ignore a boat containing hunters if there is no movement or noise.

It is worth the extra time and effort to find a good location for a tree stand (or ground stand) before hunting. Poor stand locations are seldom productive and worse, they can spook bears out of a good area or into becoming nocturnal. As with bowhunting any animal, scouting and other pre-hunt preparations greatly improve success when bowhunt-

ing brown bears. The more time prior to your hunt you allow for scouting and setting up your stand, the more likely
your scent will be dissipated and any bears will not be
spooked.

Evergreen trees (mostly spruce in Alaska) often provide good rain and wind protection for tree-stand hunters.
Bowhunters can also leave enough branches below and
around the stand to provide visual cover, but still have good
shooting lanes. The dense mat of branches above the stand
will provide good background cover. Any branches that have
to be cut to create shooting lanes should be removed from
the area. Wear rubber gloves and drag them at least thirty or
forty yards to a spot bears are not likely to travel. Cotton-
wood and birch trees are often the only choices for tree
stands, but bowhunters have to be more careful about being
spotted in these trees because these trees seldom have a lot
of branches at tree-stand height.

Tree stands should not be placed too high or the shot
angle will be too steep. A bear has a large, heavy scapula
(shoulder blade) and a thick spine that protects its heart/
lung area from a steep overhead shot. It is also difficult to
hit both lungs from a steep shot angle, and bowhunters must
get the heart or both lungs if they expect to find their trophy
nearby. However, stands should be high enough to help prevent the hunter's scent from spooking bears. Stand height
is one of those variables that has to be determined for each
situation, by using all the experience and hunting savvy you
have acquired. Ten feet is usually high enough, but higher
placements are appropriate in some locations.

Two more considerations for stand placement are the
angle of the sun and the shooting angle you prefer. A low
sun glaring off water can blind hunters to approaching bears
or prevent a good sight picture for shooting. Imagine or
actually check out the sun's angle during the time the stand

*Bowhunters must be very choosy about their shot angle with brown bears. This large boar is in a perfect position to shoot with an arrow. His near leg is forward, so the leg bone is not protecting his lungs.*

will be used. Sometimes a different tree can be selected, or the stand height can be adjusted so some nearby object will block much of the glare.

Stands must always be placed with shooting considerations in mind. Seldom should they face the most likely location for shooting at a bear. Depending on if a bowhunter is right- or left-handed, the stand should be rotated around the tree so the drawing arm does not bump the tree. A one-eighth or one-quarter turn around the tree from a facing angle is usually about right for the optimal shooting comfort.

Always practice drawing and shooting from a stand before you actually hunt. The downward angle will affect your point of impact if you have not practiced maintaining all the same tensions with your bow hand and your release hand. If you plan to shoot from a sitting position, make sure you practice that, as well as the typical standing position most bowhunters practice from. You also need to practice standing up from your seat to make sure you can do it noiselessly and without being visually detected by a nearby bear. If you are alone when hunting your stand, you should also have a backup rifle handy to dispatch any bear you strike poorly, before the wounded bear reaches the safety of the brush.

Bowhunting brown bears on carcass mounds calls for cool nerves and a good backup shooter. Bears are very protective of their food and usually alert to intruders. They will often sleep right on top of the mound so they are visible and may be approachable without waking them. However, bowhunters will probably have to wait until the bear wakes and stands up to get a good shot angle. When they are shot on their food cache, they may charge the bowhunter instinctively to protect their food.

Calling bears with predator calls is another option for bowhunters who understand and accept the risks. In fact, the first Pope & Young grizzly (2002) and brown bear (2003) that I know of being taken by women bowhunters were both brought into bow range with predator calls.

Jack Frost, who has been in on three bow-killed brown or grizzly bears, regularly practices bringing brown bears in with predator calls. His experience is that half of the bears ignore the call, and half come in to it–some slow, some faster. They will keep coming as long as the calling continues, but will stop as soon as the calling stops. He warns that callers should always be in an open spot with a 360-degree view and be very alert. He usually calls only to those bears he has already spotted so he knows which direction to watch for an incoming bear.

Bowhunters using predator calls should have backup shooters, or at least their own firearms with them at all times. Young bears or sows with cubs are just as likely to respond to these dinner bells as large, desirable trophy bears. Treestand hunters can use calls without nearly the risk of ground hunters. Continual calling for 15 to 20 minutes, which is typically necessary to bring in any type of predator, may also be necessary to bring in any brown bears.

*Stacee Meyer became the first woman bowhunter to place a grizzly bear in the Pope & Young Book with this Brooks Range bear she took in 2002. She gives credit to her father, Jack Frost, for calling the bear in, and to her husband, Rich, for giving her the opportunity.*

## SHOOTING BEARS WITH A BOW

Small kill zones, heavy muscles, heavy bones, and quick tempers all have to be dealt with when shooting brown bears with a bow. Although some large brown bears have been killed with frontal shots from bows, prudent bowhunters should wait for broadside or quartering-away shots. The dangers of following wounded bears dictate that bowhunters keep their shots well within their range of excellent accuracy.

*In 2003, Angie Ryan became the first woman bowhunter to place a brown bear in the Pope & Young Book. This bear was also called in.*

A good way to minimize the chances of wounding a brown bear is to aim no more than one-fourth of the way up the chest from the bottom of the brisket. With this aiming point, a shot even several inches high will still hit lungs, and a shot up to several inches low should still hit lungs or heart. Any shot that is too low to hit the heart should miss entirely or just nick the chest and not cause any lasting harm to the bear. By aiming a little lower than normal (for a bowhunter), you will reduce the chances of hitting too high and giving the bear a serious wound, but one that won't kill him quickly. Any low shot (that is lined up correctly left and right) will either kill the bear quickly or produce only a superficial wound to the chest. Additionally, lower shots that are too far forward or back will tend to leave a better blood trail than higher shots (with the same left-right alignment) will. Lower shots bleed better because there is less fur below them to absorb blood, and the chest or paunch cavities will start leaking fluids to make a trail before high shots would have.

One advantage bowhunters have over firearms hunters is the ability to see exactly where the arrow strikes a bear. Using highly visible fletching will facilitate this crucial element of the hunt. A backup shooter must be able to see exactly where the arrow strikes to be able to immediately decide whether or not the bear will die quickly from the hit. Bears that have been hit poorly must be immediately dispatched by a competent backup shooter.

Because this decision is so crucial to a bowhunter, the backup shooter should also be a bowhunter with plenty of experience with a bow, in addition to being a crack shot under stress. At the least, the backup shooter should view several videos showing actual kill shots to know what to look for in a good shot. Ideally, these should be bear videos. The backup shooter should not make either mistake of letting a wounded bear get away or shooting a bear that is hit well. Choose your backup shooter carefully.

Another advantage of bowhunting bears is the lack of a gunshot to alarm the bear. Gunshot bears will react violently to the bullet impact and to the noise, usually by running within seconds–if they can. An arrow-shot bear will usually react quickly by biting at the arrow and often spinning, but it will seldom run as quickly or as far without the roar of the gun to help it pinpoint the cause of its distress.

Since a bowhunter will be within a few bounds of a bear and will not have the option of using a backup gun to stop the bear (if it is to be a true bowkill), it is crucial to remain undetected by the bear. To do this, a bowhunter needs to remain as still and quiet as possible until the bear expires. Additional arrows can be shot if they are absolutely necessary and this does not alert the bear to the whereabouts of the bowhunter, but if the first arrow is definitely a heart/lung shot, more arrows may just cause the bear to flee rather than expire on the spot. It is always better to be able to keep visual contact with an arrowed bear rather than have it run into cover where it may never be found.

Some bowhunters have successfully taken brown bears without backup shooters. Some have carried heavy handguns and some carried rifles. One guide I know bowshot a brown bear from ten yards while carrying his .375 Magnum over his shoulder. He was in such a rush to swing his rifle into position after the arrow struck, he didn't even remember how his bow ended up twenty yards away in the brush.

Bowhunting for brown bears has some inherent dangers, but it does not have to be an extremely dangerous challenge. Choosing the right weapon, finding a suitable spot that doesn't put the bowhunter in extreme danger, selecting a reliable backup shooter, and recognizing your own limitations are all part of making it a successful, relatively safe hunt. You must be successful at all of these if you don't want to let wounded bears escape, or have to shoot them with a backup gun. Being in close quarters with these awe-inspiring animals is always a thrill. Meeting the challenge of bowhunting them will be a memory you will never forget.

*"To play it safe is not to play."* –Robert Altman

# 12
# TROPHY CARE

*"Dreams come true; without that possibility, nature would not incite us to have them."* –John Updike

Your dream of taking an Alaskan brown or grizzly bear has finally come true. There it lies at your feet. That huge head, those rows of long, sharp teeth operated by powerful jaws, those long, curved claws, and that powerhouse of a body. It's all there and you've done it. Now is the time to sit and reflect on all the events leading up to this moment. Record this moment's feelings indelibly into your mind to recall for the rest of your life, because life is made of a collection of memories–and this should be one of your finest memories.

## ANALYSIS
Congratulations on a successful hunt and a great adventure are first on the list. You have waited several years, or maybe most of your life for this moment, so savor it as the long-awaited achievement it is. Sit down and drink in the beauty and the wildness of Alaskan bear-hunting terrain. Wherever you may be, it will certainly be a memorable spot. Take plenty of mental pictures to store away for future years of remembering and storytelling about your hunt.

You should also use these moments to analyze what you did right and wrong for future hunts. Look at the bear's size and decide how close your estimation was and why you were accurate, or inaccurate in that judgment. Did you fail to notice any rub spots? Did you sex it correctly? Did you shoot well and at the right time? Did your weapon perform as expected? Any experience you can garner from a few moments of focused thought, while the events are still fresh in your mind, can vastly improve your future bear-hunting endeavors.

*The photo shoot is a crucial aspect of any hunt. This is a bad photo. The bear is barely recognizable. We should have taken the time to record this hunter's success properly to enjoy it the rest of our lives.*

## THE PHOTO SHOOT

The next order of business has to be recording your success on film (or on electronic media if you have a digital camera). Still photos and video footage are vital to a memorable hunt. These visual images (and maybe sounds, too) you record will help you remember some of those minor, but interesting details time may bury in your memory. Photos are as necessary for the hunter as they are for friends and family left behind who are eager to enjoy your experience as well. You owe it to them to take some time to record as many details of your experience as possible.

It helps to imagine you are a professional photographer and are being paid to take the best photos you possibly can for your client (you). Everything you do for these photos should be first-rate, as if they are a test of your ability as a trophy photographer. Would you want anything less from photos of your Alaskan brown bear hunt?

First, look around and decide what background(s) will be best for photos. In general, you should plan on taking photos from just about every angle and selecting the best ones later. Hunting gear should be placed out of sight unless there are items you want to include for a specific reason. Do not just leave gear strewn about the tundra to detract from an otherwise prize-winning photo. Make sure you take at least a few shots including your weapon and any other gear items crucial to this particular hunt.

Next, clean the bear of any blood or gore, especially around the head, which will be the focus of most photos. I try to take at least a couple photos of the animal just as I first found it, even if they will never be seen by anyone but myself (and maybe some close hunting buddies). These first photos may actually be some of the best ones if moving the animal into a better position covers it with blood or dirt that will detract from later photos. The lighter colored the animal, the more difficult it will be to remove blood or dirt for future photos. Experienced Dall sheep hunters understand this concern very well.

Next, bend, tear, break, or cut any grass, brush, or low vegetation that will block any part of the bear or hunter(s) from the camera. It is okay to take a few photos with this material still in place if your intention is to illustrate where the animal expired, but in general, these materials will just detract from the quality of your photos.

Hopefully, you know some of the basic rules of photography. If you don't, as a hunter you owe it to yourself to spend an hour or two with a real photographer (friend or professional) or at least read a photography book to learn the basics. Use the rule of thirds when placing the main subject; dead-center subjects are not as aesthetically pleasing.

Look through your viewfinder as if you are a friend back home who wasn't on the hunt and will look carefully at every piece of the photo. Is there an errant piece of gear lying on the ground? Is there a tree or bush apparently growing out of the hunter's or the bear's head? Is the hunter's face darkened by the bill from his hat? Is the bear's tongue hanging out? Is there a piece of grass stuck in the bear's lip? Is there an out-of-focus twig in the foreground catching your eye? Before snapping the shutter, take a critical look at the photo as if you are a photo judge who will notice all those little things an excited hunter/cameraman often misses when taking field photos. Take in the entire photo as you decide, don't just admire the bear through the viewfinder. If you do, you will probably take mediocre field photos at best.

I often take an hour or two to prepare and take photos of any big game trophy. After all the years of planning and anticipation, time, effort, and expense that go into a great hunt, another hour taking photos is a minimal investment. I also take at least two dozen photos, usually more, and try to use two different rolls of film, and two different cameras. These practices help insure against three possibilities–poor photography, poor developing, or a poor camera. Some situations will not allow that much time for photos, but every effort you take to preserve your hunt with good photos will be rewarded by the memories they bring back for years to come.

*This is a pretty good photo. Sometimes, photos are all we have.*

## SKINNING YOUR BEAR

If you will be hunting far from home, there are two schools of thought concerning where to take your bear for mounting. One is to bring it back to your local taxidermist whom you know, trust, and can physically go to about concerns and delays (inevitable). The other option is to leave your bear with a taxidermist in the hunting area (or state) that has plenty of experience mounting brown bears. Whichever option you choose, it should be decided before the hunt so you can talk to that taxidermist for any special instructions.

The next decision to make is what type of mount you want. This decision is sometimes dependent on what size or color bear you have just taken. Most hunters would not choose to have anything less than a nine-footer made into a full-body mount standing on its hind legs. However, a full-body mount on all four legs is a popular option for any size

*A life-size brown bear mount is impressive. The skinning procedure is virtually the same for either a full-body mount or a bear rug, so that decision can be put off until you have returned from the hunt, and had time to contemplate the cost and the space needed.*

bear. Rugs are very popular, but they do take up a lot of wall or floor space. Half-body mounts for wall displays or pedestal mounts are two more options that show the front half of the animal and don't take up as much space (nor cost as much) as life-size or rug mounts. Most taxidermists want bears skinned in the same manner, no matter what type of mount they will be made into, but it is always good to check with your taxidermist for any special instructions.

Rug mounts are the most common choice for brown bear trophies. To skin a bear for a rug mount, position the bear as flat on its back and as stretched out as you can. This will help you make the cuts in the hide as perfect as possible. Any time you deviate from the proper cuts for any mount, you may have to pay the taxidermist to sew them back together or may actually lose some of your bear's size because small amounts of hide may be trimmed to correct your mistakes.

Before you begin any skinning, lay out your knives, sharpeners, game bag(s), plastic bags, and extra rubber (surgical) gloves. I always carry several pair of surgical gloves to wear for skinning, fleshing, and salting bears. Bear hides carry lots of bacteria, so if you nick yourself, or already have an open cut, you may develop a nasty infection. Rubber or Latex gloves also keep the nasty bear grease from permeating your hands and lingering for the rest of the hunt.

Brown or grizzly bears that have been eating mainly berries and other vegetation are actually pretty tasty eating. If you have any desire to eat any meat, decide now so you can keep the meat clean as you skin the bear. Bear has a taste and texture that is different from any other animal. My wife and I love teriyaki bear (although we typically use black bear meat). For any game meat, using the powdered teriyaki marinade results in a much better flavor than the liquid kind. Brown bear has a little stronger "bear" taste than black bear, but berry-eating grizzlies can be quite good. Like pork, bear meat can carry trichinosis, so the meat must be cooked well-done all the way through to kill this potentially fatal parasite. I cook bear meat slowly, with added moisture to keep it from drying out, about twice as long as it should take for well-done meat. That way, I'm sure it has cooked thoroughly, and then some.

You will need to make five long cuts to skin a bear (see Figure 12A). I make these long cuts and do most of the skinning with my sheath knife (a Buck Woodsman). The first cut starts a few inches back of the chin, goes straight down the middle of the bear's underside, and finishes two or three inches forward of the anus. Some people make this cut from the back forward, but I always try to cut in the direction an animal's hair lies, from front to back, because I cut off less hair that way. Remember that Alaska game regulations require you to leave the external sex organs on bear hides until they are sealed by a state agent. Just go one inch to either side of the sex organ when making this first cut.

The second cut starts at the outside edge of one front pad to the middle of the chest. Make this cut by starting at the outer, back edge of a front pad, and go directly toward the elbow. Turn 90 degrees at the elbow and go through the armpit toward the middle of the chest, where you should stop when you intersect the lengthwise cut you made down the middle of the chest. Repeat this cut on the other side and finish opposite where cut number two stopped.

For the cut across the back legs, begin at the outer, rear edge of a pad on a rear paw. Go along the back edge of the leg and continue as directly as possible to intersect the spot where your first cut ended, just forward of the anus. Then start at the outer, back edge of the pad of the opposite rear paw and make a similar cut from that pad to the center cut, where you stop. You have now made the five main cuts to skin a bear.

At this point, two or more skinners can work separating the skin from the body. The closer you can skin the hide without nicking it excessively, the more fat and muscle you

## Figure 12A, SKINNING DIAGRAM

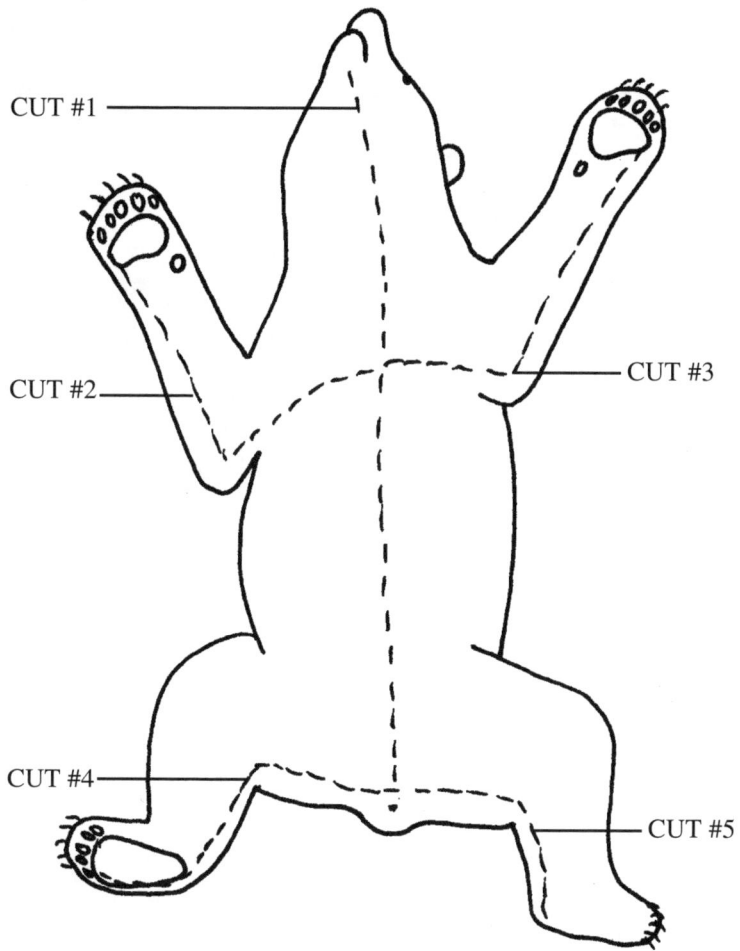

*This is the basic skinning diagram for bears–whether you want a rug or a life-size mount. Remember to start cut #1 a few inches behind the chin and end it a few inches before the anus. If you cut through all the foot pads along the outside edge and leave them attached to the hide, you can decide at a later time what type of mount to have.*

will not have to pack back to camp or have to remove later. On a large hide, the difference in weight between a closely skinned hide and one with lots of fat and muscle remaining

*Fleshing a large bear hide is a long, tedious process, but a necessary one to produce a quality trophy. The better skinning and fleshing job you do in the field, the more likely you are to have a great trophy for the rest of your life. Even an hour or two spent at a local taxidermy shop can teach a novice how to do an adequate job in the field.*

can easily be twenty or thirty pounds. Plus, the extra tissue left on the hide may take another hour or two to remove during the final fleshing process. However, if you are rushed for time (darkness or the tide is fast approaching) and the extra weight is manageable, you can remove the hide quicker by leaving an extra layer of tissue on the hide so your skinning speed is not slowed down by having to be careful about nicking the hide.

One consideration to remember when fleshing is how closely you cut to the base of the hair follicles. Hair follicles in spring hides are solidly embedded in the hide so you are not likely to cut any of these free. However, hair follicles in fall hides are not as well attached, so if you cut too close while fleshing, you may loosen some of these.

Loosened hair follicles may fall out during the tanning process and make the hair look less dense. On fall hides, watch for the bases of hair follicles appearing as you flesh and stop before you start nicking them. Leave a thin layer of flesh over them to keep them firmly embedded in the hide. You can easily see through the last thin layer of flesh so you will know when you are close and need to stop.

When you reach the rear pads, you can either go around the outside edge or go right through the middle. They will be removed for rug mounts so they do not have to be skinned carefully. However, if you want a life-size mount or may decide later that you want one, it is better to be safe and go around the outside edge of all the pads to the base of the toe pads. Then just cut across the front of the large foot pads, but behind the toe pads, to the far side (See figure 12B).

### Figure 12B. PAD-SKINNING DIAGRAM

*The dashed line shows how you should cut the pads along the outside edge, and then across the front, just behind the toe pads.*

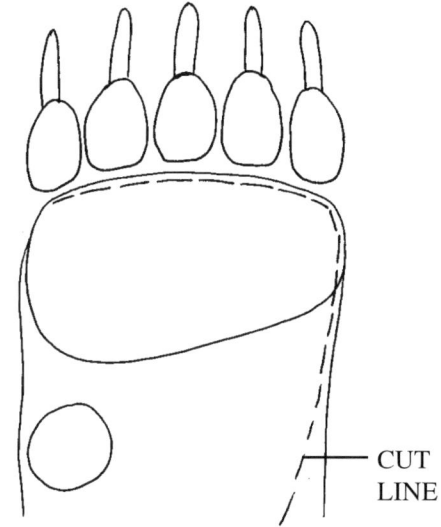

CUT LINE

This will leave the large, foot pad attached to one side and it can be flipped aside to skin the toes. Each toe bone has to be skinned all the way to the base of the claw. When field skinning, I typically just skin the feet to the base of the toes and then cut the toes (bones) off the feet. I finish skinning the toes out of the hide after returning to camp, when I can be more exact. Once you have peeled the skin off the rear legs down to the toes and cut them off, the rear legs are done for now. See the "Fleshing" section later in this chapter for instructions on finishing the toes.

The hide is then peeled off the bear from the butt toward the front legs. Upon reaching the front legs, skin them out to the paws. The front pads can be treated the same as the back pads for a rug mount. Cut along the outer edge of the front pads or cut through the middle to the base of the toes, but for any mount where the pads may be seen, cut along the outside, then across the large, foot pad behind the toes. The front toes can also be cut off at their bases like the back toes. This should free the hide all the way to the front shoulders, with only the neck and head left to do.

Before I proceed, I like to free the inner lips and the inner nose cartilage from the skull. (This can be risky if you have not tried it, so only use this time-saving procedure if you already have some skinning experience. Beginners often cut the lips with this procedure. Skip ahead four paragraphs if you don't feel comfortable with this step.) Working from the front of the skull and the outside of the mouth to accomplish this is much easier (on any animal) than trying to do it from the inside as you are coming out over the skull. I use one of the short blades (one and one-half or two and one-half inches) of my Swiss army knife for this and for most of the work around the mouth, nose, ears, and eyes.

Open the bear's mouth, pull open the lips and start cutting the skin from the lower jaw at the chin. Cut the inner, pink lips as close to the gum line as you can, leaving as much of the inner lips attached to the hide as possible. Cut directly at the bone of the jaw as you do this, with the knife's edge cutting into the jaw, not out at the hide. Work from the

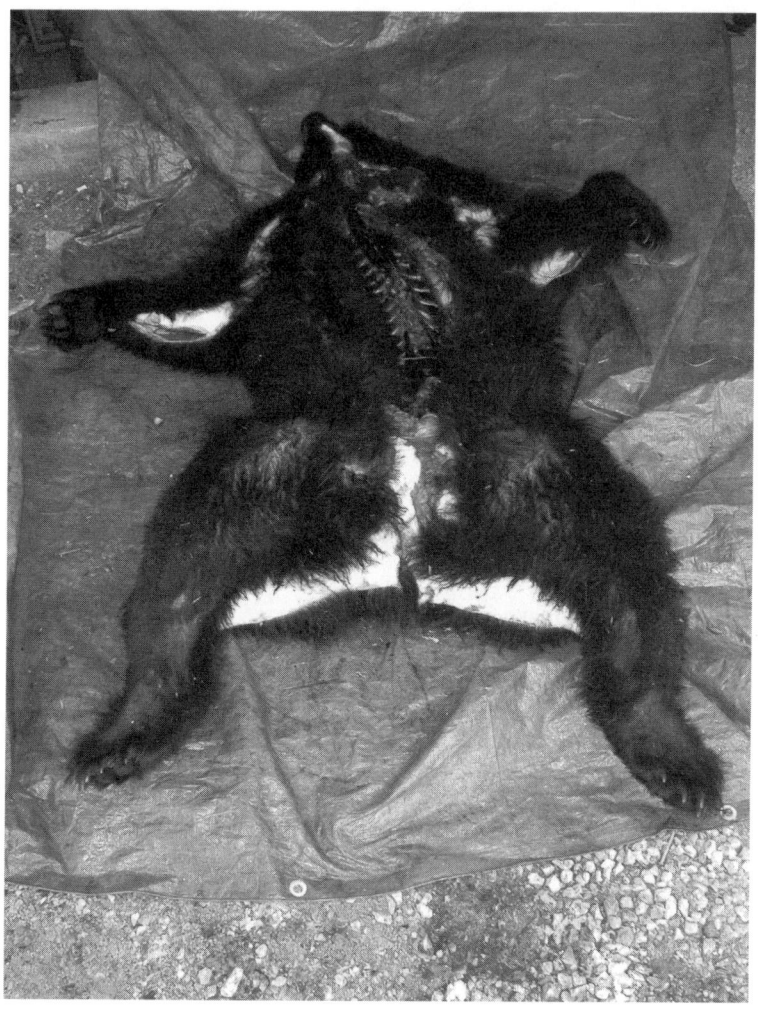

*Here is a bear with the first five cuts completed. Now, all that is left is to finish the skinning. Notice how the cuts on the legs are on the lower sides, away from the head, on both front and back legs.*

chin toward the back of the lower jaw. You will have to reach your knife inside the outer lips to get back into the corners of the mouth. If you cannot easily cut all the way back into the corners, you can leave those cuts until you skin the hide over the head.

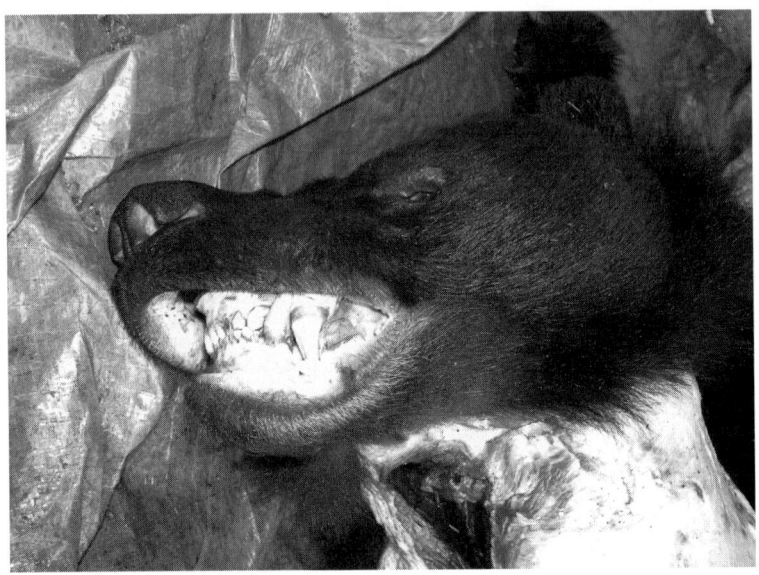

*If you have enough experience, you may cut the gums free from the jaw bone before skinning the hide over the head. In this photo, I have already cut upper and lower gums free from the jaw. Note that there is at least one inch of inner gum left on the hide. Leave as much inner gum attached to the hide as you can.*

After both of the inner cuts have been made on the lower jaw, the chin will be free and hanging down from the skull. These cuts you've made to free the inner lips of the lower jaw should actually connect (from the inside) with the very first cut you made on this bear from the outside of the chin.

Now you can free the hide from the upper jaw and the top of the snout. Begin by opening the mouth, grasping the upper lips and lifting upwards. This should expose the inner lips around the upper jaw. Begin by cutting the inner, pink lips in the front, just below the nose, and again try to free them and leave as much inner lip attached to the hide as possible. Cut back along both sides of the upper jaw toward the corners of the mouth and then as far as you can reach inside the corners. With the upper lips free, lift them

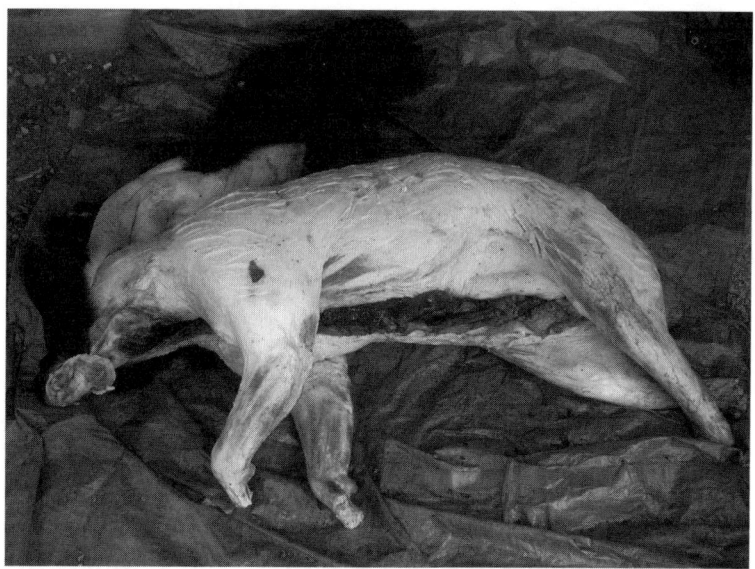

*The hide has been skinned all the way to the back of the head, the gums have been separated from the jaw, and the hide is ready to be pulled over the head so the skull can be skinned out.*

and the nose up as much as possible to view the inner nose cartilage. Cut this cartilage off from the front as close to the bone of the upper skull as possible. As you get toward the back of the nose cartilage, just before you have it completely free, be very careful. Ease up on your knife's pressure and don't go too far or you will cut through the hide on top of the snout. Leave as much cartilage as you can on the hide. Leaving more nose cartilage on the hide will make it easier to turn the nose later, and easier for your taxidermist to create a realistic-looking nose on your mount.

Now that the chin and the nose are free from the skull, you can resume skinning the hide up the body of the bear. (If you did not feel comfortable starting from the front of the skull earlier in my explanation, this is where you would begin after all the feet were done.) Skin over the neck and pull the entire hide up over the head so it is out of the way to finish skinning the head. When you reach the ears, you must cut very deeply into the muscle of the head and leave as much ear cartilage as you can on the hide, for the same reasons as you left the maximum amount of nose cartilage on the hide. Follow the ear cartilage down toward the skull until it is less than one inch wide, or smaller, before you cut it off the skull. If you cut off the ears too far out, you will end up leaving part of the ears on the bear's skull. You will need to use the point of your knife for this job as the ear cartilage lies between thick layers of jaw muscles and actually begins right at the skull. If your knife touches the skull as you cut off the ear cartilage, you have done well.

After the ears are detached from the skull, the next crucial task is removing the hide around the eyes. Skin the hide away from the skull forward until you are close to the rear corner of the eyes. From the outside of the hide poke a finger (of your non-knife hand) into the rear corner of the eyelid. Use this finger as a guide to prevent your knife from cutting into the eyelid. Carefully work your knife to separate the hide from the skull around the eye. There is only a thin tissue that attaches the eyelid to the bone around the eye, so be careful with the knife. As you separate the eyelid from the back corner and move toward the front, it will be more closely attached. The front corner of the eyelid is attached in a little depression in the bone around the eye, so you must use the tip of a blade to carefully cut it free. Always cut into the skull so any slip doesn't cause your knife to cut into the hide. In these tricky areas around the face, just make tiny nicks in the tissue that holds the hide to the skull and keep tension on the hide with your off hand. If you just make tiny cuts toward the skull, you will slowly remove the hide and shouldn't make any major mistakes.

After the eyelids are separated from the skull, all that is left are the nose and gums—most of which you have al-

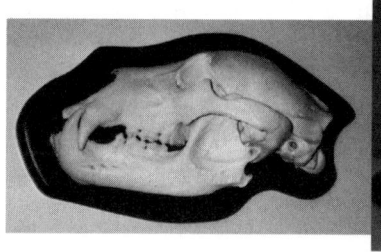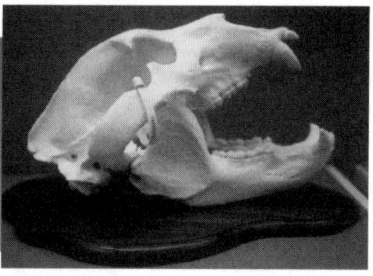

*These two skull mounts depict two unusual options for a trophy display–a half-skull mount on the left, and an open-mouthed skull on the right.*

ready separated from the outside before you started the head. As you continue pulling the hide over the head and separating it from the skull, you should see the inside corner of the gum lines that were not quite cut free from the outside. Cut these against the skull just as you did from the front and continue until you reach those earlier cuts. The hide should now be completely free from the body and skull.

The next task to finish before leaving the kill site is to tag your bear hide. There are a few GMU's (Game Management Units) in Alaska where resident hunters do not have to tag brown bears, but in most of the state it is still required. All *nonresident* hunters must place their locking tags on the hide before moving the bear from where it was killed. Find or make a small hole near the edge of the hide (the anus works well), push the metal locking tag through this hole, and then lock the two ends of the tag together. This only takes a few seconds, but if you fail to do this simple task, you can be cited and fined.

Lay the hide fur side down, fold the legs inward, fold the hide in half lengthwise, then roll the hide up starting at the head. This will help protect the fur on the head from any physical abrasion during transport back to camp. It is convenient to have a large, strong game bag (I sew mine out of cotton muslin and add a drawstring) at this point to drop the rolled hide into. Then, I put this bag into a plastic bag to prevent blood from soaking my pack and getting through to my back during the trip back to camp.

If you do use plastic bags at any time with your hide, be extremely careful as they can ruin a hide by retaining heat and moisture. Do not leave the hide in a plastic bag any longer than necessary for packing or other short periods of time to protect it. If you use black plastic bags, the sun will heat them up quickly and you can ruin your hide in a few short hours. If you are at all uncertain, don't use plastic around your hide.

The weight of a fresh bear hide (without the skull) is surprisingly heavy. Depending on how closely the hide was skinned and how much extra tissue was left on it, an eight-footer will weigh about 60 pounds, a nine-footer about 80 pounds, and a ten-footer–120 pounds and up. Some large bear hides can weigh over 150 pounds. Packing even the smaller hides to camp can be a real test of strength and stamina, and you will be glad for every extra ounce of tissue you removed during the skinning process. Some very heavy hides have been cut in half in order to get them back to camp. If there is absolutely no other way to get an enormous hide back to camp than by cutting it in half, be sure and cut it lengthwise, down the middle of the back (starting to one side of the head) where the hair is the longest. If the hide must be cut, at least your taxidermist will have the thickest, longest hair to cover up his sewing line.

One more fact to consider is that some brown bears will have lice on them. This is more common with southeastern coastal bears, but could occur anywhere. To avoid getting lice on yourself, always use a pack or put the hide in a sack before carrying it any distance. This will also prevent your clothes from absorbing the smell of the bear, which is a very distinct odor that is very difficult to remove. Most

*A happy hunter with a great hide represents a lot of hard work, and skill–both in the hunt and in the field care of the hide.*

guides have a set of clothes and even raingear specifically for bear hunting because of this strong, resistant odor bears impart to anything that touches the hide or skull.

## FLESHING AND SALTING

Once you have returned to camp, you must take care of the bear hide properly or it may spoil. The raw hide may actually begin to rot immediately if neglected. The two factors that cause the most damage are heat and moisture. In a warm, moist environment, bacteria grow rapidly and raw tissue begins to break down rapidly. The first rule is to always keep any raw hide as dry and as cool as possible.

The next steps to care for your hide will be to remove excess flesh and fat from the hide, turn the ears and nose, split the eyes and lips, and salt the entire hide to help dry it. These procedures are very difficult to explain in words, and still photos don't really depict how to accomplish these tasks. The best advice I have is to go see any taxidermist, hopefully yours, and watch them flesh a hide. The same techniques are used on bears as on any game animal for fleshing, turning, and splitting the hide and facial region. The only aspect of a bear you cannot learn from hoofed animal skins is how to turn the toes. However, your taxidermist can show you how to do this on a bear (or any canine hide) or other animal mount that has toes and claws. There is no substitute for an in-person visit to a taxidermist, and I have never met one who didn't welcome his clients to come down and learn the right techniques to prepare a hide for mounting.

All excess flesh and fat must be removed from the hide, face region, and toes to prepare the hide for the next step–salting. Any excess flesh or fat will prevent the salt from drawing out moisture–which may then cause hair slippage or spoiling of the hide. You will need at least 15 to 25 pounds of fine salt, depending on the size of your hide and how efficiently you use the salt. Once the hide is completely fleshed and all the correct parts turned and split, lay the hide fur side down on a flat surface. It is very handy to have an extra tarp for this step. It will keep the hide cleaner and drier, plus let you catch and reuse any salt that goes over the edge of the hide.

Salt for hides must be fine-grained, not rock salt. If you have selected a taxidermist to mount your bear, they will often give you enough salt to take care of a bear hide. Pour a small pile of salt on the hide, spread it out, and rub it in well. The facial features, the feet, and the cut edges are all crucial areas that need extra attention and salt. The edges of the hide have a tendency to curl inward and stick together. This little folded area has to be opened and salted so it will dry. Otherwise, the hair may slip (fall out) from these edges and these hairless strips of hide will have to be trimmed by the taxidermist. The result will be a smaller rug mount when it is all finished.

Once a liberal amount of salt is rubbed onto every single square inch of the inner hide surface, it should be rolled in the same manner as for packing. Fold the legs in first, fold the hide in half lengthwise, then roll the hide from the head to the tail. The salted, rolled hide should be stored on a dry surface (elevated and slanted is preferable) in the coolest spot available where it will not get rained on. Remember, the salting process is intended to dry the hide, so protect it from any additional moisture. During this time, fluid that the salt has drawn from the hide will drain out of the rolled hide. This is normal and exactly what you want to happen. If you can place the rolled hide on a slanted surface, it will drain better and not sit in its own fluid. Prevent anything of value from getting soaked with this smelly, bear liquid as it will be almost impossible to get the smell out.

Let the hide sit for 24 to 48 hours, then unroll it and hang it or lay it out to drain off any excess moisture. After it drains, re-salt the hide and roll it up again using the same procedures as the first time. If you are short of salt, you can brush off the used, wet salt, let it drain of fluid so it is dry, and then reuse it on the hide. You cannot salt the hide too much (unless it gets so stiff you can't bend it to put it in the plane). If the hide has been fleshed and salted properly so it is dry, you should have no problems keeping it for a week or more in the field. This is partly dependent on temperature and humidity. Always keep the hide out of the sun and away from any source of heat or moisture, as those are the factors that will ruin the hide.

The way you care for your bear hide from the moment you start shooting until it is delivered to your taxidermist will have a significant effect on the finished mount. It always helps to read about what procedures you are not familiar with, or a little familiar with, but not an expert at. However, receiving some hands-on instruction from a taxidermist on proper field care of your brown bear trophy will be invaluable to you as a big game hunter. Most of these same skills you acquire to care for a brown bear hide will be useful when caring for any animal hide. It is an important part of your skill base as a knowledgeable big game hunter.

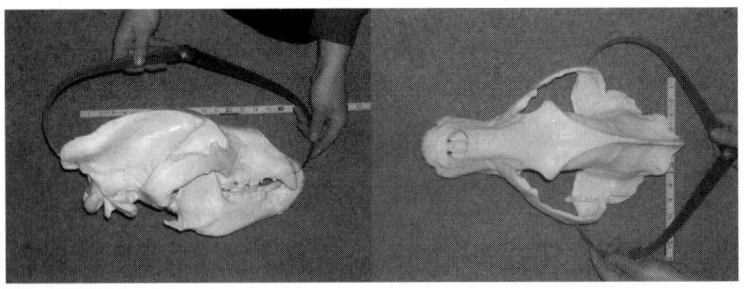

*To score bears, the length and the width of their skulls is measured with calipers to the nearest 1/16 of an inch. The score is the sum of the two measurements.*

*"Some folks never exaggerate–they just remember big."*
–Audrey Snead

# 13
# BEAR SAFETY

*"One of the most dangerous forms of human error is forgetting what one is trying to achieve."* – *Paul Nitze*

Bear hunters don't want to just kill a bear, they want to hunt for and have the opportunity to take a big bear. They do not want to be forced to kill aggressive bears just to protect themselves. Since bear hunters try to find areas with high bear concentrations and then put themselves in close proximity to these bears, they will (hopefully) have numerous bear encounters during each hunt. If they do not understand and practice bear safety, they may be exposing themselves to unnecessary bear attacks that could end in personal injury or the needless death of an undersized or In-Defense-of-Life-and-Property (DLP) bear.

## DLP BEARS

In-Defense-of-Life-and-Property (DLP) bears can be killed "to protect your life or property if you did not provoke an attack or cause a problem by negligently leaving human or pet food or garbage in a manner that attracts wildlife and if you have done everything else you can to protect your life and property" (1, ADF&G, 2002). The hide and skull of a DLP bear become the property of the State of Alaska and must be turned in within 15 days. As bear hunters, we should know enough about the animals we hunt to avoid situations where we add to the number of DLP bears killed each year in Alaska.

*The largest percentage of DLP bear killings involve sows with cubs. The cubs don't know enough to stay away from humans, so the sows have to protect them, which causes most of the bear problems. If you ever see a cub, you know the sow is nearby, so act accordingly.*

Statewide, about five percent of the brown bears killed each year by humans are DLP bears. About ten Kodiak bears are killed each year as DLP bears (6, ADF&G, 2002). These bears are subtracted from the number of bears available for hunting. DLP bears are more likely to be young bears and/ or females, which have an even more significant effect on the overall population of brown bears available for hunters each year.

Only one person has been killed on Kodiak Island in the past 70 years (as of 2002) and statewide, brown bears killed 13 people in the twenty years from 1980 to 1999 and injured 75 others (6, ADF&G, 2002). However, the number of DLP bears increases right after a bear attack appears in the media. We bear hunters should understand enough about our quarry and do everything we can to avoid this overreaction and any unnecessary DLP bears.

# BEAR COUNTRY ETIQUETTE

Unwanted bear encounters are those where you have to shoot a small or illegal bear, or come close to doing so. Because bear hunters put themselves in the middle of bear habitat, there is always this possibility of having to shoot an undesirable bear. However, your behavior in bear camp and on your daily hunts will have a significant effect on the likelihood of such an encounter.

Most of the basics of living in bear country without attracting unwanted bears pertain to food. There are many do's and don't's about handling food in bear country:
- whenever possible, do not cook in your sleeping tent;
- store foods away from your sleeping tent;
- use smell- and bear-proof containers for food storage;
- hang foods from trees when necessary and possible;
- use foods that cook quickly and produce minimal odors;
- cook and eat where you have a good view of any approaching bears;
- dump cooking and dishwashing liquids away from your sleeping tent;
- don't bury food leftovers–bears will dig them up;
- don't burn food-containing garbage unless you can burn it completely and are about to leave–bears are attracted by the smell of the burning food;
- seal garbage tightly in plastic bags and store it out of reach of bears;
- toothpaste attracts bears, treat it like food;
- and once a bear gets a taste of food or garbage from your camp, plan on it coming back for more.

Many of these activities concerning food may attract bears, which may seem like a good thing to bear hunters. However, it is illegal to bait bears with food or anything they like (they are attracted to kerosene and diesel fuel spills). Plus, the bears most likely to come into a bear camp

*Bears travel with their heads down because they are using their excellent noses to find food odors. If you have food in the Alaskan outdoors, any nearby (downwind) bear will smell it. Take the appropriate precautions.*

looking for your smelly food are young bears and sows with cubs–neither of which are desirable trophies. Any respectable bear hunter looking for a decent trophy should keep a clean camp and handle food so it does not attract nuisance bears.

Hanging food and other desirable substances from trees is a good way to keep it out of the reach of bears. In general, items should be hung fourteen feet off the ground and four feet away from a tree trunk. Although brown bears reportedly cannot climb trees because of their long claws, there are exceptions to this rule.

A group of bowhunters I know were on their annual blacktail deer hunt on Kodiak. They had strung a wire cable between two trees, thrown a rope over the cable, and used this to hoist their food and their deer out of the reach of bears. One night, after this food cache had been molested two nights in a row, one of the hunters stayed awake to catch the perpetrator. To his surprise, a large brown bear slipped into camp, climbed and pulled itself up one of the supporting trees, shimmied out on the cable, and chewed through one of the ropes holding a deer carcass.

They nicknamed the bear "Einstein" for solving the seemingly impossible problem of a steel cable, and just had to live with its nighttime, feeding visits until they finished their hunt. At least it was old and wise enough to come at night to avoid those pesky humans with their loud guns. This story just shows you what lengths bears will go to when they smell food–even though it is in a camp full of hunters.

In addition to the basic rules about food handling in bear country, there are several general rules about how to act in bear country:

- •bears do not like surprises so always remember this whenever you are in bear country;
- •keep dogs on a leash when bears may be near, and better yet, leave them at home;
- •have your partner keep watch whenever you are cleaning an animal, even a bear, in bear country–a hunter bending over a kill is an open invitation for another bear to move in and claim the carcass;
- •make noise regularly whenever you are in bear country and you don't want to see a bear at close range;
- •and if you must walk bear trails at night, be alert and ready to deal with a close-up, surprised bear.

As bear hunters, we will not always follow these rules. However, if we know the rules, we can minimize the risks we take around bears by following most of them whenever it is practical.

## CLOSE ENCOUNTERS

Bears are intelligent, curious, and potentially dangerous. They must always be treated with those characteristics in mind. Like many species, bears have developed social patterns and behaviors to limit the number of life-threatening encounters they have with each other. Knowing these behaviors will enable hunters to have close encounters with bears without undue risk to themselves or the bears.

Most bears will avoid people if they can. If you have a close encounter with an undesirable bear (undesirable means you don't want it as a trophy) that sees you, always observe the bear closely for clues to its mood and its next actions. A large bear that has seen people many times will most likely make a quick exit. However, a large bear that may be the king of the local woods may not even be alert to its immediate surroundings. Some large bears don't feel threatened by anything, so they may not even notice you until you are very close. This is one of the reasons to always be alert on narrow, brushy trail–especially at night. You can stumble into one of these large, dominant bears at close range and have only seconds to decide on the best mode of action.

Young bears are much more likely to be curious (your bear-judging skill becomes important here as you quickly size up the bear to decide how to handle this situation). They are more likely to come toward you to find out what you are, and if you are food. They also may not understand that humans are a real threat, so you may have to educate the bear with loud noises and anything that can scare the bear without harming it.

Sows with cubs present the greatest danger of attack. Sows do not like anything or anyone threatening their cubs and are quick to go on the offensive when this happens. One of the worst situations to be in is coming between a sow brown bear and her cubs, particularly if the cubs get

*Bears are excellent swimmers so a little river is no obstacle. This sow is looking toward the camera as if she is interested in something on this side of the river. If a bear already sees you and still decides to come look for food, it will be a problem bear as long as you stay in the area. They seldom leave once they smell food.*

scared and decide to bawl for mamma. She will come running, and if you are in the way, you have to react quickly.

Whenever you encounter a bear, the first observation you should make is whether it has seen you. If it hasn't, and its travel route will keep it more than 100 yards away from your position, the safest action is to just let it continue on its course. If it is going to smell you along its route, that is fine. You may hear a sudden commotion as the bear woofs and then maybe some crashing if the brush is thick, as the alarmed bear runs away from your scent.

If the bear is going to come closer than 100 yards along its travel route, you have to consider the other aspects of the situation. If it is a larger bear (still not the one you want to shoot) or a young bear, and it will get your scent before it gets within 50 yards, you should just let it continue until it smells you and then probably runs off, but stay alert to its reaction, either by watching it or listening if it goes out of sight.

If a sow with cubs is going to come within 100 yards of you before it scents you, things are different. If the cubs are first-year cubs and are staying close behind mamma, it is probably okay to let her continue and then get your scent within 100 yards, but outside of 50 yards. If a sow with older cubs—which often stray and are not timid creatures—is coming that close, you may consider alerting her to your presence. If you are alone and a sow with large cubs will pass by within 100 yards and not spot you, it may be best to let them go. If you are with one or more partners, you may want to alert the bears to your presence before they get any closer. Sows with large cubs often act together as a team, and if any one of them decides to charge, they all come at once. It is often better to let them know you are human(s) before they commit to a charge. If you are alone, without one or more partners to make a show of strength, you have less chance of intimidating a team like this.

If a bear or bears are going to come very close or already are close to you and haven't spotted you yet, it is better to alert them to your presence before they get really close. The reasons to do this are so you don't surprise them at close range, you let them know you are not one of their prey species, and you can give them plenty of room to retreat rather than charge. By letting bear(s) know you are there before they get too close, you give them an easier way out of a potentially threatening situation. If you let them get too close, they may feel more threatened (particularly if it is a sow with cubs) and charge as a defensive action.

If you have decided to let a bear know of your presence to prevent a closer, sudden encounter, the idea is to make them aware of what you are and that you are not threat-

*Bears that are habituated to humans—which often happens on popular fishing streams like this one—are still as dangerous as 'wild' bears, if not more. These photographers have taken the recommended precautions–their bear rifle is lying on the tundra within easy reach.*

ening their cubs or their food. Always stand up tall, raise your arms to make yourself appear larger, speak loud enough for them to hear you clearly, and step from side to side so they can see you are human. You should appear deliberate and unalarmed in your actions, but make sure the bear knows you are human. Their eyes are not the greatest so by stepping back and forth, they are more likely to quickly identify you as human and decide to leave.

Never turn your back on a bear unless you are positive you can reach a 100 percent safe location, like a building or automobile, before the bear can reach you. If you do turn your back on a bear, the odds are it will chase you just like an aggressive dog will chase you if you run from it. A bear is always looking for food, so if you run, it will chase you to see if you are a food item and, if you are not food, you must be a competitor for food so it will want to establish its dominance by chasing you away.

*Under normal circumstances, this is my favorite view of a sow with cubs–they are leaving my vicinity in a relaxed manner.*

If you are in a group of hunters, always stay together and side by side so the bear sees every one of the group. Bears' social behavior is based on bluffing more than actual fighting among themselves. You always want to show how many of you there are in the group, how calm and unafraid you are, and how large you are. If you are alone, waving your arms or even waving a tarp or a backpack, or anything that makes you appear larger, will make a bear think you are too much for it to handle.

Just last fall, on one of my solo brown bear scouting trips, I spotted three little cubs about 80 yards away–crossing in front of me. The brush was fairly thick so I didn't have a good view all around me and had no idea where the sow was. The cubs didn't see me, but I didn't want the sow to suddenly appear close to me and think I was molesting her cubs. I had my bear rifle so I decided to yell and wave my arms to alert the cubs. They immediately saw me and ran off in the direction they were headed. I heard a loud woof and then the upset sow appeared, looking for whatever scared her cubs. She saw me and immediately recognized I was human (because I was waving and yelling), and wheeled off to run away with her cubs right behind her.

I could have let the cubs continue on without spotting me, but I wasn't sure where the sow was and didn't want her to surprise me at close quarters. Also, I wouldn't have known which way to go to avoid her since my return trip that day would have been on the same route as the cubs'. In these types of circumstances, I usually alert the bears so I don't have any surprises later on that day. If it was a single bear at 80 yards, I would have let it go by and just watched its direction and actions carefully.

## THEIR MOODS

Whenever you have a close encounter with a bear that you don't want as a trophy, observe its body language carefully to make the best decision about your course of action. Bears' body language is similar in many ways to that of dogs. A staring bear with its head up and lifted ears that makes no sound is probably trying to figure out what you are and deciding what to do. Bears that stand up on their hind legs are also trying to figure out what you are. This is the perfect time to make yourself appear large and human so it can decide to leave.

A bear that lowers its head, lays its ears back, and stiffens is angry and aggressive (just like a dog with this appearance). If you give this bear the slightest reason to charge, it will. With this type of bear, it is even more important for you to do only those things that make you appear human and unafraid. Never turn your back on this type of bear or sit or squat, which will make you appear small and vulnerable. These actions on your part will invite a charge.

On one of my Kodiak deer bowhunts, one of our group ran into a bear that kept coming at him across the open tundra. This bowhunter turned his back and tried to walk away from the bear, which just made the bear more determined to follow him. When the bear got within about fifty yards, the bowhunter sat down on the tundra so he looked small and vulnerable. The bear kept coming so the bowhunter shot it with a twelve-gauge he carried for that purpose. By walking away and sitting, the bowhunter was just inviting the bear to come after him.

Woofing sounds from a bear usually mean a surprised bear or an uncertain bear, but it may also mean an upset bear. A bear that makes sounds like barking, moaning, bawling, or roaring is indicating you are too close and it is uncomfortable. This bear may be about to charge. A bear that swings its head from side to side, walks sideways while staring at you, makes yawning motions, or paws the ground is also undecided and may be about to charge. If you can, angle away from this type of bear or back up very slowly to give it more room, but never turn your back and definitely don't run. At times like these, I always have a shell chambered and my safety off.

A bear that makes a deep gargling sound, a low growling sound, or pops its teeth is even more likely to charge. These are the stickiest of situations and require you to do everything you can to give the bear an easy way out and not provoke it. If the bear's mood and actions seem to be worsening, you may have to resort to making louder noises and being more aggressive, but always maintain your human qualities. Don't try to act like an aggressive bear or that may provoke a charge.

## TOO CLOSE

If all these standard bear defenses haven't worked and the bear is coming closer or charging, there are a few more things to remember. First, bears bluff charge much more

*Young bears like this will sometimes get too close for comfort. They are inexperienced, curious, and looking for food. They are also very powerful, dangerous animals when they get excited.*

than they actually make contact during a confrontation. In fact, some experts believe all bear charges are bluffs if you do not run. Bears want to make their adversary (or quarry) run by using intimidation. If a bear encounter has gradually progressed to this stage, or you are suddenly faced with a charging bear, your option of running to the safety of a building or automobile is long gone. So, you have to stand your ground–always. Most of the time, this will stop a charging bear, and it will eventually leave. Bears may bluff charge up to a few feet and still turn away and leave. However, if you have a good bear weapon, it is not prudent to let a bear come that close in hopes it will only bluff, particularly if it comes at you very fast, with laid-back ears, with little noise, in the manner of a real attack (just like an attacking dog would).

The distance at which you decide to shoot is up to you, but it should be well inside 100 feet. For one thing, you will be hard pressed to even hit a charging bear farther than 100 feet, let alone place the bullet accurately. Shooting charging bears outside of 100 feet will probably result in wounded bears that are just bluffing 99 percent of the time.

On one of my solo moose hunts on the Kenai in the 70's, I spotted a brown bear at about 100 yards, coming right at me. He was walking like he was king of the woods without a care in the world. I got into a small, fifty-foot opening and yelled to let it know I was there. The bear picked up its head, looked at me, and started running–right at me. I chambered a cartridge and waited. At about 100 feet, it veered off into the brush and ran within about fifty feet of me, but concealed by the brush. I heard it stop, and pause, then it came right at me again, only to veer off again before it actually got to me.

I just stood my ground and listened. The bear tried running right at me one more time, and when I wouldn't run (as it had hoped), it just veered off again and continued on its way through the woods, not quite king anymore. That bear was just trying to get me to run so he could eat me if I was prey, or establish his dominance if I was a competitor. I wouldn't run, so his bluff didn't work. I'm positive if I would have run, he would have ran after, and caught me.

If an attacking bear is close and you are not prepared to shoot it (no weapon in your hands or no time to point it), throw anything you have toward the bear. Charging bears will tend to hit anything at this moment, and your pack or water bottle may just slow them enough for you to get your gun ready or take other evasive action.

If you do have to shoot a bear at close range, be prepared. As Keith Johnson, a notable brown bear guide, says, "...any pistol is a poor weapon against a brown bear." (Unpredictable Giants). Stopping an attacking brown bear at close range with the most powerful handguns made is diffi-

*The best weapon for bear protection is the same rifle you would choose for a bear hunt. Handguns and shotguns are okay, but nothing beats a good bear rifle in which you have confidence.*

cult even in the most expert hands. Twelve-gauge shotguns may be slightly better weapons for this purpose, but their soft slugs don't penetrate as well as dangerous-game bullets from a heavy caliber rifle. Bear hunters should be carrying a heavy caliber rifle with a well-constructed bullet anyway, and that is what you would want to use to stop an attacking brown bear.

If you do have to shoot an attacking brown bear at close range, there are a few key points to remember. A fast-moving, head-on bear does not present a good target. If its head is low, try to avoid hitting the top of the skull, as the heavy bone may deflect the bullet. If possible, it is best to shoot through the nose, the open mouth, or through the front of the neck to reach the brain or spinal cord of the neck. Hitting either should kill the bear immediately.

If you can't hit either the brain or the spinal cord of the neck, the next best shot will be right next to the neck at its base, angling into the chest area to strike the lungs or heart. If you only have time for a snap shot, and you are trying to gain time for a better placement, or for your partner(s) to get their guns on the bear, you may only succeed in slowing the bear down by breaking the bones of the shoulders and/or front legs–with the plan to immediately get more shots into the animal. Attacking bears usually come fast, giving you little time to think of a plan. As a bear hunter, you need to have this all thought out so you will instinctively react in the best manner to stop the bear. Wherever you aim or hit the bear, you should plan on working the rifle's action and firing as fast as you can; don't just shoot once and then pause to see what happened–keep firing until you are out of shells, then reload and be ready to do it again.

If an attacking bear actually reaches you, the best defensive position for you to be in is a tightly curled ball with your head protected. The bear will most likely want to slap you around or bite you a few times to show its dominance. If you lie still and quiet, it will probably walk off after it feels you are no threat and it has established dominance. If you make noise or move while the bear can still hear or see you, it may come back to teach you another lesson.

If a bear reaches you and a weapon is near at hand, you may not want to go for the weapon. Unless you are sure you can get off at least one good shot before the bear can reach you, moving may just provoke another attack or increase the intensity and duration of the current attack.

If a bear attacks and doesn't stop or is biting your head, your life is on the line so you may decide to fight back. I have read about one man who actually won a battle with a large brown bear by using only a knife, but few of us could do that successfully. Like most animals, bears' noses are tender spots so if forced into physical combat, the nose and the eyes are the places to aim your blows with your hands or any weapon you can find. The chances of winning such a battle are slim, but may be the only chance if you run into a rare predatory bear or one that doesn't appear to be stopping after you play dead.

Most brown and grizzly bears avoid people whenever they can. Food is the most common reason people have problems with bears. Even if food is involved, bears do not necessarily have to be killed just because they show up in camp.

During one solo trip to the Wrangell Mountains, I was waiting near a makeshift strip for my pick-up plane. One morning I slept in and was dozing in my small backpacking tent. As I was just waking up, I remember hearing sniffing and snorting sounds outside the tent, just a few feet from my head. I just lay there and let the bear walk away. When I looked outside, there was a three- or four-year-old grizzly playing with the surveyors' tape I had tied on a bush to indicate wind direction for my pilot. The bear was unconcerned I was there, made a wide circle around my tent as he looked for food, and then just ambled off down the runway.

Another time on the Alaskan Peninsula, I had this obnoxious bowhunter who had no respect for the brown bears I was guiding him for. He kept insisting I was afraid of them because I was careful whenever we spotted fresh cub tracks in the sand or spotted a sow with cubs coming our way. He saw no reason to be cautious–he wasn't afraid of no "bar." I taught him to respect bears one night.

We were camped in an eight-by-eight Bombshelter (tent) along a salmon-filled creek. There were plenty of salmon in our creek and in the many nearby creeks. Each night the client would go to sleep right after dinner, but I would lie in my sleeping bag and read by lantern-light. On several nights I heard bears walking by the tent, and even investigating our cooking area about 100 feet away from the tent. However, the bears were well-fed with salmon and never bothered our food or gear. I had not told the client about these late-night visits since there wasn't a problem.

On the eighth night of the hunt, after the client fell asleep and I was still reading, a bear came up to the foot of the tent and was sniffing and grunting–just being a curious bear. It was pitch black outside so we couldn't hunt until daylight, but I woke the client anyway and said, "There's your bear. He's within bow distance." As the client became more awake and realized there was a brown bear just a few feet from the foot of his sleeping bag, his eyes got really big. I had the only rifle lying next to me so he pulled out this small pocketknife with a three-inch blade and held it so tight, his knuckles turned white. I continued reading for a while, then turned out the lantern, but the client was still sitting up in his bag, with a death-grip on his tiny knife.

After that hunt ended, without the client getting a bear, we were sitting and waiting for our pick-up plane. At that point the client acknowledged that since the night when I pointed out his bow-range brown bear, he hadn't slept a wink–in three days! It took him one entire hunt, but he had learned to give brown bears the respect they always deserve.

Brown bear hunters with a good understanding of their quarry and how to react during close encounters should not have to kill DLP bears, except in very rare cases. We should always be alert for bears, observe them very closely for clues to their moods, react accordingly to avoid threatening behaviors on our part, know the best ways to show them we are humans and we are not afraid, never run or tempt bears with food, and know what to do in the very rare case of an actual attack.

I have been enjoying the Alaskan outdoors for over forty years and have had hundreds of bear encounters, but have never even had to shoot *at* a bear in self-defense. The odds are very good I won't have to do so in the next forty years I spend in the Alaskan outdoors. As bear hunters, it is in our best interest, and the bears', that we take every reasonable precaution so we don't ever have to kill a DLP bear.

*These two bears are feuding over a fishing spot and they both have the scars to prove they are not afraid of a fight. It is fascinating to watch bears, particularly when they interact with other bears. Just keep a respectable distance, keep a watchful eye out for sows and cubs, and keep your gun with you. We keep reading about people who say this isn't necessary, but when we read about these people who say this, it is often in an article about a bear attack–and an obituary. Bears are unpredictable, so allow for that, and go ahead and enjoy the Alaskan Outdoors.*

*"Anyone can make a mistake. A fool insists on repeating it."* –Robertine Maynard

*Waiting for lunch.*

# 14
# OLD SNAGGLE TOOTH
# by Jack Frost

*"How we spend our days is, of course, how we spend our lives."* –Annie Dillard

Stalking a wounded Alaskan brown bear with a gun is hazardous enough, but doing so with a bow and arrow is more conducive to an exciting life than a long one. Nevertheless, I was determined to follow through and complete the job that I had started an hour before when I first shot an arrow at this great bear. A steady 20-knot wind and open, slightly rolling tundra had enabled me to keep the wounded bear in sight and to close in on him, slowly and silently. The bear was big—at least nine feet—and although he had lost quite a bit of blood from the arrow wound, he was far from dead. Only 20 yards of bare tundra separated us as I drew my 73-lb. compound bow for what I hoped would be the final shot. At the twang of the bowstring, the bear whirled from his bed to charge. The moment of truth had arrived.

I had been an avid hunter for over thirty years and a serious bowhunter for the past eight, so a move to Alaska from Pennsylvania in 1973 had been a hunter's dream come true. I spent my first few years trying to kill (with a gun) at least one of each of the big Alaskan animals that I had spent so many years reading about. As I learned more, Alaskan game became easier to harvest. I felt that some of the challenge had gone out of hunting, so I turned to bowhunting.

For me, hunting with a bow put the challenge and excitement back into hunting. I believe the best quality time in hunting is that interval between initially spotting a game animal and either making the kill or spooking the animal. With a rifle, that high-quality time interval of being "with" the game is frequently rather short, but with a bow, the same time interval is frequently very long.

My first good opportunity to hunt brown bear came in 1980, when I drew a permit to hunt on Unimak Island. Although I was unable to find a backup gunner to accompany me, I decided to go anyway. In a week on the island by myself, I saw 26 bear but killed no bear on that trip. In the spring of 1985, I was again fortunate enough to draw a permit to hunt on Unimak Island. In addition, my good friend Tony Oney had some free time and a desire to see if an arrow could kill a brown bear. Tony is one of the few men in whom I would have the confidence to back me up in an attempt to kill a big bear with a bow. We made plans to each fly our Super Cubs down to Unimak Island for the hunt.

While flying the beach in search of bear sign on the first day, Tony found a dead whale on the beach and two large bears nearby. We found a place to land our planes and camp a few miles down the beach from the dead whale. The next day we moved into position to hunt. While glassing one of the bears, I noticed he had a lower tooth sticking out at an odd angle, like the tusk of a boar. I had heard about "Old Snaggle Tooth" and now, here I was, face to face with him.

Our stalk brought us to a bluff about 50 yards from the dead whale where the snaggle-toothed bear was feeding. It was a perfect setup, but I wished the bear was a little closer. Everything seemed to be under control, but I was reluctant to shoot at 50 yards, especially with a stiff breeze blowing. When the other large bear appeared on the beach headed for the whale, the snaggle-toothed bear stopped his feeding and headed for the approaching bear. With Tony's prompting, I decided now was the time to shoot. I drew my 73-lb. "Grand Slam" bow, held the 50-yard pin on the bear, and shot. The arrow hit high—just behind the shoulder—and the bear turned and ran down the beach, while the other bear claimed the whale. The snaggle-toothed bear went 200 yards along the beach, turned inland about 150 yards and then lay down on the open tundra.

Over the next 30 minutes the bear made several beds in the same area, never staying in a bed more than a few minutes. The bear began to lie still for longer periods in the next half-hour so we decided to try to get close enough for a killing shot. We got about 20 yards from the bear when it looked directly at us–he knew we were there. After a moment, he turned and looked away. I drew and shot, the arrow burying itself to the fletching just behind the shoulder. With amazing quickness, he whirled from his bed to charge. I knew he was dead but I was afraid I might be too, before he realized his own demise. He looked immense–fur standing out, ears laid back, snaggle-tooth fangs bared. But there was no charge. He just stood there, then his mouth closed, his eyes glazed, and he settled back into his bed–dead.

The last arrow was squarely through the heart. The previous arrow had hit the backbone, but didn't break it and did not get inside the chest. There is no doubt in my mind that, had I missed the heart on my last shot, there was plenty of strength left for the bear to do me some real damage. Before fleshing, the bear was nine feet, ten inches wide and nine feet, nine inches long. Normally, a bear is squared after fleshing, and I believe he would have gone ten feet at that time. The biggest surprise came when I picked up the boiled and bleached skull from the taxidermist. After the required 60-day drying period, the skull was officially measured at 28 3/16. This is 3/16 larger than Fred Bear's world record brown bear taken in 1960. So my bear is possibly a new world record; it depends on how the panel of Pope & Young measurers score it at their next convention. I must admit it would be neat to have number one, but Fred Bear is one of my real heroes and it is somehow fitting that he should have the number one bear. In the final analysis, I don't care how it turns out. The size of the skull had nothing to do with the excitement and thrill of the kill, and no one can take that thrill away from me. (Editor's note: Jack Frost's bear is currently tied for #1 in the P&Y Book.)

*Jack Frost with 'Old Snaggle Tooth.' What a memory to have–meeting an old, seasoned veteran of many fights on open tundra, with only a bow and some sharp sticks. This is the thrill of* **Bear Hunting in Alaska.**

*"I have failed over and over again in my life. And that is why I succeed."* —Michael Jordan

# REFERENCES

1.) Alaska Department of Fish & Game. "Alaska Hunting Regulations No. 44," ADF&G 2003

2.) —. "Bears and You," Alaska: ADF&G, 2001

3.) —. "Brown Bear," –Wildlife Notebook Series, Alaska: ADF&G, 2002

4.) —. "Brown Bear Fun Facts," Alaska: ADF&G, 2001

5.) —. "Living in Harmony with Bears: Bears and 'Food'," Alaska: ADF&G, 2002

6.) —. "Kodiak Bear Fact Sheet," Alaska: ADF&G, 2002

7.) —. "The Essentials for Traveling in Bear Country," Alaska: ADF&G, 2002

8.) Bartely, Bruce, Conversation on 1/07/2004, ADF&G Biologist.

9.) Blauwkamp, Terry. "Do You Need a New Rifle this Fall?", *Game Trails,* Fall 2002

10.) Boddington, USMC, Col. Craig. "World Class Bear Hunts," *American Hunter,* April 2001

11.) Byers, C. Randall and George A. Bettas, *Records of North American Big Game*, United States of America, Boone and Crockett Club,1999

12.) Donnelly, Kathleen. "Bad News for Bears," *Backpacker,* September 2002

13.) Fithian, Robert. "Tribute to Wofgang Kuper," *The Alaska Professional Hunter,* Winter 2003

14.) Gilchrist, Duncan. *All About Bears,* Hamilton, Montana: Outdoor Expeditions and Books, 1989

15.) Hanback, Michael. "The Art of the Draw," *American Hunter,* November 2003

16.) Holt, Rob. "A Hunting Story," *The Alaska Professional Hunter,* Winter 2003

17.) Howe, Steve. "Gust Busting," *Backpacker,* September 2002

18.) Johnson, Keith N. *Unpredictable Giants: 40 Years of Alaskan Brown Bear Hunting Tales,* Glenwood Springs, Colorado: Gran Farnum Printing and Publishing, Inc., 2001

19.) Matheny, Mark. *Bear Safety Tips,* Bozeman, Montana: UDAP Industries, 2002

20.) McMurphy, Larry. Conversation on 2/7/2004, Woodland Taxidermy, Palmer, AK, 907-745-1134

21.) Nordberg, Dr. Ken. *Do-It-Yourself Black Bear Baiting and Hunting,* Minneapolis: Bear Hunting Publications, Inc., 2001

22.) Robb, Bob. "There are no Atheist Grizzly Bear Hunters," *Safari,* March/April 2003

23.) —. "Giant Bruins," *American Hunter,* August 2002

24.) Runyon, Wendell. "Grizzlies are Tough," *The Alaska Professional Hunter,* Winter 2003

25.) Simpson, Layne. "Lessons from 85 Dead Brown Bears,"*American Hunter,* April 2002

26.) Stonorov, Derek. *Living in Harmony with Bears,* Homer, Alaska: National Audubon Society, 2000

27.) *Take a Closer Look,* Yukon Government Renewable Resources, Keyah Productions, 70-minute video

28.) Tilton, Buck. "A Fast Fix for Fatigue," *www.Backpacker.com,* May 2001

29.) Towsley, Bryce M. "Tips for Traveling Hunters," *American Hunter,* February 2003

# RECOMMENDED READING

*Sheep Hunting in Alaska: The Dall Sheep Hunter's Guide, 2nd Edition*, Tony Russ, Wasilla, Alaska: Northern Publishing, 2002.

*The Manual for Successful Hunters: Why 10% of the Hunters Take 90% of the Game*, Tony Russ, Wasilla, Alaska: Northern Publishing, 1999.

*Alaska Wear:  The Visitor's Guide to Clothing*, Tony Russ, Wasilla, Alaska: Northern Publishing, 2001.

*Conditioning for Outdoor Fitness*, David Musnick, M.D. and Mark Pierce, A.T.C., Seattle, WA, The Mountaineers, 1999.

*Boomers Really Can Put Old on Hold*, Barbara Morris, R.Ph., Escondido, CA, Image F/X Publications, 2002.

*Strength Training Past 50*, Wayne L. Westcott and Thomas R. Baechle, 1998.

*Staying Fit Over Fifty*, Jim Sloan, Seattle, WA, The Mountaineers, 1999.

*The Complete Walker IV*, Colin Fletcher & Chip Rawlins, New York, NY, Alfred A. Knopf, 2002.

*Stretching*, Bob Anderson, Bolinas, CA, Shelter Publications, Inc., 2000.

# PHOTO CREDITS

Bob Ameen - p.224

Boone & Crockett - map p.24, scoring form p.287

Carl Brent - pp.95, 97, 101, 120, 161, 170

Robert Cassell - for helping my wife to find bears to
            photograph

Chris Cork - p.98

Jack Harrison - pp.109, 131, 169, 228, 273

Susie Heuer - pp.33, 166, 181, 219, 260, 268, 278

Mark Keller - pp.49, 133, 153, 188, 197, 223, 246, 255

Larry McMurphy - p.258

Mark Mitten - pp.34, 37, 39, 144, 163, 191, 193

Mark Niver - pp.29, 165

Matt Reisterer - p.242

Rene Russ - pp.22, 30, 141, 172, 176, 186, 199, 201, 207,
            211, 213, 217, 231, 265, 267, 271

Andy Savland - p.89

Jim Stocker - p.255

Jody Walker - pp.27, 182, 262

Mark Walker - p.86

George Wescott - Front & Back Cover Photos, pp.57, 91,
            93, 103, 137, 154, 227

All other photos by Author

*Thanks to everyone who donated photos for this
project. These photos make the book more than just my book,
it is our book. I really appreciate your help. –*Tony Russ

# Boone & Crockett bear scoring form

Records of
North American
Big Game

250 Station Drive
Missoula, MT 59801
(406) 542-1888

## BOONE AND CROCKETT CLUB®
### OFFICIAL SCORING SYSTEM FOR NORTH AMERICAN BIG GAME TROPHIES

**BEAR**

|  | MINIMUM SCORES | |
|---|---|---|
|  | **AWARDS** | **ALL-TIME** |
| black bear | 20 | 21 |
| grizzly bear | 23 | 24 |
| Alaska brown bear | 26 | 28 |
| polar bear | 27 | 27 |

**KIND OF BEAR (check one)**
- ☐ black bear
- ☐ grizzly
- ☐ Alaska brown bear
- ☐ polar

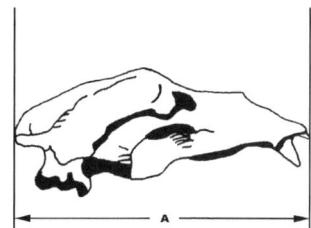

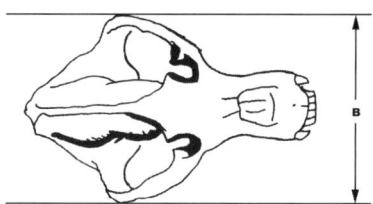

| SEE OTHER SIDE FOR INSTRUCTIONS | MEASUREMENTS |
|---|---|
| A. Greatest Length Without Lower Jaw | |
| B. Greatest Width | |
| **FINAL SCORE** | |

Exact Locality Where Killed:

Date Killed: _____ Hunter: _____

Owner: _____ Telephone #: _____

Owner's Address:

Guide's Name and Address:

Remarks: (Mention Any Abnormalities or Unique Qualities)

I, _____ , certify that I have measured this trophy on _____
　　　　　　　PRINT NAME　　　　　　　　　　　　　　　　　　　　　　　　　　　　MM/DD/YYYYY

at _____
　　STREET ADDRESS　　　　　　　　　　　　　　　　　　　CITY　　　　　　　　　STATE/PROVINCE

and that these measurements and data are, to the best of my knowledge and belief, made in accordance with the instructions given.

Witness: _____ Signature: _____ I.D. Number [ ][ ][ ][ ]
　　　　　　　　　　　　　　　　　　　　　　B&C OFFICIAL MEASURER

# Index

## Symbols

.270 Winchester, 194
.30-30 Winchester, 194
.30.06, 194
7mm Magnum, 194

## A

ABC islands, 25
Afognak Island, 23
after the shot, 218
Alaska Department of Fish &
    Game, 40, 88
Alaska Game Regulations, 88
    Alaskan guide, 90
        veteran bear guides, 177
    baiting bears, 261
    "cub" definition, 90
    evidence of sex, 90
    external sex organs, 244
    sealing officer, 89
Alaska Peninsula, 13, 14, 21, 28,
    32, 41, 48, 91, 99, 127, 172,
    183, 275
    Peninsula, 100, 124, 126, 132
Alaskan Outdoors, 277
Alaska's bowhunting laws, 225
analysis, 237

## B

beach stalks, 164
beached whale, 38, 280
bear attacks, 13, 260
bear blind, 122
bear calibers, 191
    .300 H&H Magnum, 187
    .300 Remington Ultra Mag.,
        194, 196
    .338 Winchester Magnum, 18,
        192, 193, 196, 198, 212
    .375 Winchester, 212, 236
    .416 Remington, 192, 193
bear condo, 14, 125
bear country etiquette, 261
bear dens, 136
    denning spots, 136
bear hunting gear, 59
bear hunting seasons, 90
bear sizes, 171
bear-proof container, 261
bears' eyesight, 161
behavioral characteristics, 31
    dominance hierarchies, 33
    hierarchial social structure, 33
biological classification, 21
    Ursus arctos, 22
    Ursus arctos middendorffi, 22,
        39
black bear, 30
bluffing, 268, 272
    bluff, 271
    bluff charge, 270
    body language, 269
Bodyglide, 62
Bombshelter, 70, 275
BOOK ORDER FORM, 294
Boone & Crockett, 57, 86, 87,
    91, 95, 99, 101, 102, 133,
    157, 171
    scoring form, 171
Boone and Crockett Club, 23
bowhunter, 97, 115, 149, 225,
    228, 236, 270
bowhunting, 225, 279
    bowhunting methods, 226
    broadhead, 226
        mechanical broadhead, 226
    equipment regulations, 225
    peak draw weight, 226
    shot angle, 230

Brooks Range, 28, 102, 127, 159, 233
brown bear tags, 89
brown bears, 21
Buck Woodsman, 76, 244
bullet construction, 197
    well-constructed bullet, 273
bullet placement, 191

## C

Cabela's Waterfowler's Parka, 66
calibers & bullets for bears, 191
calipers, 258
camouflage, 68
camping, 69
    bear camp, 107
    carbon monoxide poisoning, 113
    deadman anchors, 114
    food odors, 114
    ground cloth, 71
    pitching camp, 111
    sleeping bags, 72
    sleeping cots, 71
    stove selection, 72
    Weatherport, 73
    where to camp, 108
    wind funnel, 114
cannibalism, 36
carcass, 263
carcass mound, 143, 144, 149, 165, 232
Chicagof Island, 89
close encounters, 264, 269
clothing, 65
    commercial fishing gloves, 67
    layering, 65, 122
    neoprene face masks, 68
    scent-blocking, 116
    white suit, 68
Cold Bay, 78
cruising shorelines, 38, 145

## D

Decelerator pad, 194
diet, 37
digital camera, 238
disposable handwarmers, 78
diurnal, 32
DLP bears, 259, 276
drawing permit areas, 92
drawing-only system, 91

## E

ear cartilage, 252
eating, 114
eating well, 54
    energy/protein bars, 54
    energy window, 168
elevated stand, 228
extreme tides, 148, 220

## F

fall hides, 94
Flatlander from Georgia, 51
fleshing and salting, 255
    fleshing, 246
food sources, 138
fooling their ears, 162
foot pad, 247
    front pad width, 178
footwear, 62
    leather boots, 63
    overboots, 67

## G

game management units (GMU's), 90
GEAR CHECKLIST, 83
GORE-TEX, 66
GPS, 76
grizzly bear, 21, 87, 102, 132, 159, 187, 227, 232
    mountain grizzly, 108, 209

Ursus horribilis, 22

## H

habituated bear, 267
hair follicles, 246
hair slippage, 256
half-body mount, 242
handgun, 272
head wagging, 33
hibernation, 29, 35, 36
hip boots, 41, 162
  ankle-fit boots, 62
  boot-fit models, 62
hypothermia, 65

## I

Impertech raincoat, 66
initial analysis, 155

## J

judging size, 173
jump-shooting, 15

## K

Kenai Peninsula, 22, 272
kill zone, 189, 203, 206, 211
knee-high rubber boots, 63
Kodiak Archipelago, 21, 28, 39
Kodiak brown bear, 39, 86, 91,
  103, 105, 133, 146, 153,
  172, 215, 220, 222, 260
Kodiak Island, 26, 31, 36, 75,
  87, 99, 119, 127, 145, 167,
  260, 262, 269
Kodiak National Wildlife
  Refuge, 40

## L

lice, 254
life history, 35
  breeding, 35

delayed implantation, 36
life-size brown bear mount, 242,
  245
skinning procedure, 242
locking tag, 253

## M

make a plan, 157
mating season, 130
mental readiness, 41, 56
Mulchatna, 98
muskeg, 49
muzzle brake, 194
muzzleloader, 196

## N

nickel-plated, 196
nocturnal, 32, 96, 124, 127
Nokia, 62
nonresidents, 88, 101, 106, 202
nose cartilage, 248, 251

## O

*Old Snaggle Tooth*, 280
omnivores, 118, 139
one-second rule, 208, 212
one-shot kill, 210, 214
optics, 59
  binoculars, 59
  objective lenses, 60
  Swarovski, 60
Other trophy considerations, 183

## P

photo shoot, 238
  field photos, 240
physical training, 41, 43, 54
  cardiorespiratory condition-
    ing, 43
  stamina training, 43
  strength training, 43, 48

stretching, 45, 48
  joint mobility, 45
  stretching for flexibility, 43
  wake-up stretch, 46
places to hunt, 98
plastic bag, 254
polyurethane, 66
Pope & Young, 232, 282
Pope & Young Book, 233
Pope and Young Club, 25
powder bottle, 158, 228
predator call, 232
predatory bear, 275
Prince William Sound, 100

**Q**

quill bears, 128

**R**

range of brown bears, 25
range sandbag, 195
rangefinder, 76
recovery and refueling, 167
registration permit, 87, 92
remain alert, 164
rifle scope, 198
rubbed hides, 184
rug mount, 242, 247, 257
rule of thirds, 240

**S**

Safari Club International, 25, 98
salmon streams, 140, 149, 228
scent contamination, 228
scent trails, 108
scoring bears, 258
second degree of kindred, 88
sex determination, 179
  HEAD SHAPES, 180
  neck length, 181
shooting bears, 201
  BEAR ANATOMY, 205

shooting bears with a bow, 233
spinal cord, 273
shooting sticks, 200
shot angle, 205, 217
shot placement, 206, 208, 218, 274
shotgun, 273
sixteen reasons to keep shooting, 189
SIZE RELATIONSHIPS CHART, 178
skinning your bear, 241
  eyelid, 252
  PAD-SKINNING DIAGRAM, 247
  SKINNING DIAGRAM, 245
skull mount, 253
snowmachine hunting, 151
snowshoes, 74, 152
  Sherpa snowshoes, 74
sports-related injuries, 46
spot and stalk, 118, 167
  spot and run, 122
spotting bears, 118
spotting knob, 14, 19, 110, 120, 125, 129, 167
spring hides, 94
spring hunting, 130
squared hide size, 173
stainless, 196
stamina, 51, 254
stand-hunting, 149, 150
  elevated stand, 150
subsistence seasons, 92
sunblock, 79
synthetics, 65, 124
  polypropylene, 65
  Powerstretch Polartec, 65

**T**

Talkeetna Mountains, 29, 209

tanning process, 247
taxidermist, 241, 251, 257
teeth-popping, 33
  popping, 18
teriyaki bear, 243
their moods, 269
thermals, 158, 160
Thinsulate, 66
Toklat grizzly, 28, 182
too close, 270
traveling with gear, 80
travois, 78
trichinosis, 243
trophy classification, 23
trophy quality, 92
turn the ears, 256
twelve-gauge, 270

## U

ungulates, 38, 190
Unimak Island, 24, 100, 280

## V

vegetarian, 37

## W

walking, 52
waterproof binoculars, 59
whale carcass, 143
wounded bear, 279
  wounded bear procedure, 220
Wrangell Mountains, 127, 275

# TONYRUSS.COM

*Guiding you to Success in the Alaskan Outdoors*

## <u>ORDER FORM</u>

*All books are fully refundable; satisfaction is guaranteed.*

**Sheep Hunting in Alaska - 2nd Edition,** by
    Tony Russ, Softcover-$22.95, Hardback-$29.95
**Bear Hunting in Alaska**, by Tony Russ,
    Softcover-$22.95, Hardback-$30.00
**Moose Hunting in Alaska**, by Rich Hackenberg,
    Softcover-$22.95
**The Manual for Successful Hunters**, by Tony Russ,
    Softcover-$24.95, Hardback-$30.00
**The Quest for Dall Sheep**, by Jack Wilson,
    Softcover-$19.95
**The Johnny Luster Story**, by Mary E. Adams,
    Softcover-$19.95
**Alaska Bowhunting Records**, by Tony Russ,
    Hardback-$15.00
**Alaska Wear**, By Tony Russ,
    Softcover-$15.95

**BOOK TOTAL**..................................... $_____
**SHIPPING by air** ($5 for 1st book, $2
each additional book, International -        $_____
approx. double these fees) ...................
**TOTAL ENCLOSED** ......................... $_____

Name:_____

Address:_____

City:_____State:_____Zip:_____

Telephone:_____

email address:_____

Send check or money order to Northern Publishing, P.O. Box 871803, Wasilla, AK 99687. Or visit **www.TonyRuss.com** to order with a credit card, plus see our other products and services. Contact us at tony@TonyRuss.com.

# TONYRUSS.COM
*Guiding you to Success in the Alaskan Outdoors*

# ORDER FORM

*All books are fully refundable; satisfaction is guaranteed.*

**Sheep Hunting in Alaska - 2nd Edition,** by
Tony Russ, Softcover-$22.95, Hardback-$29.95
**Bear Hunting in Alaska**, by Tony Russ,
Softcover-$22.95, Hardback-$30.00
**Moose Hunting in Alaska**, by Rich Hackenberg,
Softcover-$22.95
**The Manual for Successful Hunters**, by Tony Russ,
Softcover-$24.95, Hardback-$30.00
**The Quest for Dall Sheep**, by Jack Wilson,
Softcover-$19.95
**The Johnny Luster Story**, by Mary E. Adams,
Softcover-$19.95
**Alaska Bowhunting Records**, by Tony Russ,
Hardback-$15.00
**Alaska Wear**, By Tony Russ,
Softcover-$15.95

**BOOK TOTAL**.................................... $_____
**SHIPPING by air** ($5 for 1st book, $2
each additional book, International -         $_____
approx. double these fees) ...................
**TOTAL ENCLOSED** ......................... $_____

Name:_____

Address:_____

City:_____State:_____Zip:_____

Telephone:_____

email address:_____

Send check or money order to Northern Publishing, P.O. Box 871803, Wasilla, AK 99687. Or visit **www.TonyRuss.com** to order with a credit card, plus see our other products and services. Contact us at tony@TonyRuss.com.